# ELIJAH
# EZRA AND NEHEMIAH
# SCHOOL

Group's hands-On BiBLE curriculum™

## Grades 1 and 2
## Summer
## Teachers Guide

Group
Loveland, Colorado

# Group

**Hands-On Bible Curriculum™, Grades 1 and 2, Summer**
Copyright © 1995 and 1997 Group Publishing, Inc.

First Printing, 1997 Edition

**Credits**
**Contributing Authors:** Cindy Dingwall, Lori Haynes Niles, and Liz Shockey
**Editor:** Beth Rowland Wolf
**Managing Editor:** Paul Woods
**Chief Creative Officer:** Joani Schultz
**Copy Editor:** Candace McMahan
**Art Director:** Helen H. Lannis
**Cover Art Director:** Helen H. Lannis
**Designers:** Jean Bruns and Dori Walker
**Computer Graphic Artist:** Rosalie Lawrence
**Cover Photographer:** Craig DeMartino
**Illustrators:** Ken Bowser, Bill Fisher, Vicki Logan, and Jennifer Skopp
**Audio Engineer:** Steve Saavedra
**Production Manager:** Ann Marie Gordon

Unless otherwise noted, Scriptures quoted from The Youth Bible, New Century Version, copyright © 1991 by Word Publishing, Dallas, Texas 75039. Used by permission.

ISBN 0-7644-0032-0
Printed in the United States of America.

# CONTENTS

Aug3

# H·O·W T·O U·S·E T·H·I·S B·O·O·K

## WHY HANDS-ON BIBLE CURRICULUM™?

There's nothing more exciting than helping children develop a relationship with God. But teaching first- and second-graders about God can be a challenge. It's difficult to find activities that work with readers and nonreaders. It's hard to explain abstract truths that many adults may not understand. Some children have been in church since birth and appear to know it all. For others, learning about God is brand-new. Teachers tell us they're desperate for something that works.

We've found a way to get children excited to learn about God. Each quarter of Hands-On Bible Curriculum™ is packed with fresh, creative, *active* programming that will capture children's interest and keep them eager for more.

Here's why Hands-On Bible Curriculum will work for you.

## A NEW APPROACH TO LEARNING

Research shows that children remember about 90 percent of what they *do* but less than 10 percent of what they *hear.* What does this say to us? Simply that children don't learn by being lectured! They need to be actively involved in lively experiences that bring home the lesson's point.

Group's Hands-On Bible Curriculum uses a unique approach to Christian education called active learning. In each session, children participate in a variety of fun and memorable learning experiences that help them understand one important point. As each activity unfolds, children discover and internalize Bible stories and biblical truths. Because they're *doing* instead of just listening, children remember what they learn.

Your children will be fascinated with the neat gadgets and gizmos packed in the Learning Lab®. And you'll feel good about seeing children grow spiritually while they're having fun.

To build excitement, keep the contents of the Learning Lab under cover. Children will be curious about what wonderful gizmos will appear in next week's lesson.

All the activities are designed to work with classes of any size, although we recommend having at least one teacher for every 10 children. The items in the Learning Lab may be used in several lessons, so be sure to hang on to them.

In each lesson you'll find a photocopiable "Growing Together" handout to send home with children. Besides providing an important link between home and church, the "Growing Together" handout features great art projects, family activities, prayers, and parenting tips to help parents reinforce the point of the lesson at home. You can encourage parents' involvement during the next 13 weeks by mailing photocopies of the parents letter found on page 11. All the pages in the teachers guide are perforated to make your job easier. Just tear out the photocopiable pages and make as many photocopies as you need for your class.

The items listed below are typical supplies that may be used in the lessons in this book. All other items required for teaching are included in the Learning Lab. We recommend your children use their own Bibles in this course so they can discover for themselves the value and relevance of the Scriptures.

- cassette player
- chalkboard and chalk
- construction paper
- crayons
- glue or glue stick
- markers
- masking tape
- matches
- newsprint
- old magazines
- old newspapers
- paper clips
- paper cups
- pencils
- plain paper
- scissors
- snacks
- stapler
- 3×5 cards
- transparent tape
- trash cans

# UCCESSFUL TEACHING: YOU CAN DO IT!

What does active learning mean to you as a teacher? It takes a lot of pressure off because the spotlight shifts from you to the children. Instead of being the principal player, you become a guide and facilitator—a choreographer of sorts! These ideas will get you started in your new role:

● **Be creative in your use of classroom space.** Move your tables aside so children can move around freely and work in groups. Have chairs available but be willing to sit on the floor as well. Chairs can be a distraction, and moving them around slows down your lesson.

● **Think about open areas in the church.** These places might be available for activities: the foyer, the front of the sanctuary, a side yard, or parking lot. Children love variety; a different setting can bring new life and excitement to your lessons.

● **Be sure to help children tie each experience to The Point of the lesson.** Every activity in each lesson is designed to teach a specific point. It's important to repeat The Point over and over during the lesson to make sure children hear it and learn it.

Studies show that people need to hear new information up to 75 times to learn it. You may think you're being redundant, but you're actually reinforcing The Point and making sure children see how it applies to their lives. Whenever you can, repeat The Point during the lesson just as it's worded. You can even have the children say it with you to make sure they know it.

● **The gizmos from the Learning Lab are exciting to children.** Keep distractions to a minimum by gathering the gizmos before class discussions.

● **Focus on discussing the activities with children.** Don't skip over the discussion in favor of doing more activities. The activities allow children to *experience* biblical truths. And the discussions teach children how to *apply* the experiences to their lives. The printed discussion questions and summary statements will help children explore their feelings, discover important biblical principles, and decide how to apply these principles to their lives. But if your class is large, don't think every child must answer every question. Children will learn from those who share even if only two or three answer each question.

● **Ask—don't tell.** As you lead discussions with your class, ask open-ended questions rather than rephrasing questions as statements and asking children to agree. Your children will learn much more about God if they make the discoveries about the Bible themselves. Trust the Holy Spirit to teach them.

● **Read the suggested responses.** With each discussion question, we've included answers your children may give. These aren't meant to tell you what the "right" answers are but simply to prepare you for what children might say. Don't worry if children give "wrong" answers. They need to have freedom to explore. They'll learn from the answers other children give.

● **Don't forget to use active listening.** Ask, "What did you mean?" Say, "Tell me more." These techniques will cause children to explore their beliefs and learn more about God. They'll also give you a chance to get to know children better and find out what they know.

● **Keep children excited with the Learning Lab gizmos.** Children are intrigued by the items we've chosen to show them how Scripture is relevant to their lives. Keep children interested by only showing the Learning Lab items as each one is used in the lessons. This way, there will be a new and exciting discovery each week.

● **Remember that children learn in different ways.** So don't shy away from an activity just because you've never done anything like it before. It may be just what's needed to help one of your children get The Point.

● **Get to know your children.** When you meet your class members for the first time, get to know them by name. Ask a fun question such as "If you were an animal, what would you be and why?" to help everyone get to know one another.

And when new children show up from week to week, welcome them to the class and help them feel at home. Your sincere interest in each class member will greatly enhance the experiences you'll share in the next 13 weeks.

● **Know your children's abilities and needs.** Refresh your memory on what it was like being a first- or second-grader by scanning the chart on page 10. It will help you know a bit more about the needs, wants, and abilities of the children you'll be teaching during the next 13 weeks. Be sensitive to children with special needs. Check with parents to see how best to help them. Remind kids that all believers are part of the family of God and have special abilities to offer.

● **Make your class a "safe zone" for children with special needs and learning disabilities.** Avoid calling on children to read or pray aloud if they find it embarrassing. Pair good readers with nonreaders, and both will benefit.

● **Capitalize on your children's strengths.** A student who doesn't read well may be a terrific song leader for your class. A shy, introverted student may have wonderful insights and the ability to resolve problems. When you're forming groups, put active children with quiet, thoughtful children. Learn to let your children shine by drawing on their strengths and allowing each of them to make positive contributions to the class.

● **One of your strongest teaching tools is affirmation.** Children need to know that their contributions are important. Call children by name. Recognize their strengths. Compliment them for Christlike behavior.

● **Try pairing children who know the Bible with children who don't know the Bible.** Let them teach each other. If children know a Bible story so well they lose interest while you tell it, turn the tables and have them teach *you* the Bible story. You might be surprised at how much they know.

● **Let children teach each other.** Don't be hesitant to have children work together in small groups for discussions and projects. They'll learn valuable skills to help them work with others. And often, what they learn about God sticks in their minds better when they've learned it from a classmate. The teachers guide gives you many opportunities to have students work in small groups, but use this technique any time to teach children to express their faith to one another.

● **Wait at least 30 seconds for children to respond when you ask a question.** Try offering a controversial answer to spark more responses. Or tell your children to take a few seconds to think of their answers, then call on one child by name to begin the discussion.

● **If your children can't seem to stop talking,** use the attention-getting signal, then tell children it's time to wrap up the discussion and move on.

● **If your children seem restless, take a break.** Burn up their excess energy with action songs or jumping jacks. Then lead a few stretches and return to the lesson. For more ideas, try *Fidget Busters: 101 Quick Attention-Getters for Children's Ministry.* It's available from Group Publishing, P.O. Box 481, Loveland, CO 80539.

● **Be aware of the attitudes children bring into class.** Some children may walk in after fighting with their siblings or being reprimanded by their parents. Encourage them to share their feelings, then be patient as they work to overcome their bad day.

# ATTENTION, PLEASE!

Stand back and get ready for a radical idea: Noise can be a good thing in Sunday school! Educators will tell you that children process new information best by interacting with each other. Having children quiet and controlled doesn't necessarily mean your class is a success. A better clue might be seeing happy, involved, excited children moving around the classroom, discussing how to apply to their lives the new truths they're learning.

There is a difference between good and bad noise. Good noise is learning noise—children discovering and sharing new insights. Bad noise is disruptive and destructive. Put an end to bad noise by using the attention-getting signal and separating students who egg each other on.

If noise and activity can be good, how does a teacher keep control?

Good question! And we've got some good answers.

● **Keep things moving!** Most children have about a seven-minute attention span—the amount of time between TV commercials. That means you need to be ready to move on to the next activity *before* children get bored with the current one.

● **Establish attention-getting signals.** Flashing the lights or raising your hand will let children know it's time to stop what they're doing and look at you. You'll find a suggestion for a signal in the introduction to each module. You can use this signal throughout all 13 weeks. Rehearse the signal with your children at the beginning of each class. Once your children become familiar with the signal, regaining their attention will become an automatic classroom ritual.

● **Participate—don't just observe.** Your enthusiasm will draw children into an activity and help them see you as a person, not just someone in authority. Get down to children's eye level so they don't think of you as a giant but as an accessible, caring friend.

● **Look for teachable moments.** Sometimes an activity will look like it didn't work. Or maybe something entirely unexpected will happen. But children can learn from an activity that seems like a flop. An activity that seems to be a flop may provide a wonderful opportunity for learning if you ask questions such as "Why didn't this work out?" "How is this like what happens in real life?" or "What can we learn from this experience?"

● **Adjust the lessons for your class.** When options are given, use one or both of them. Use the Bonus Ideas beginning on page 161 to lengthen the lesson. You can also use the Out-of-the-Box Ideas that are listed in some lessons to lengthen a class session. These ideas require supplies that aren't included in the Learning Lab. Each lesson is complete without the Out-of-the-Box Ideas, but these extras are lots of fun when you want to do something more.

The lessons can also be shortened. If you have a large group or a short class session, pick three or four of the activities that will work best with your children. If you make The Point during each activity, you'll have taught something significant even if you don't get through the whole lesson.

● **If you're running short on time, skip to the closing.** Every activity teaches Bible truths, but the closing usually includes prayer and a commitment to action. The closing activity will solidify the lesson's point and provide a wrap-up for the lesson.

● **Adapt the lessons to your class size.** While each activity works with larger classes, the bigger the class size, the more time the activity will take. But don't worry; children will get the main point in every activity. They'll have caught the lesson aim even if they don't do every activity.

● **Use the Fidget Buster.** It's a lively activity designed to help children burn up excess energy, then settle down quickly and focus on the lesson.

● **Use the Time Stuffers.** These independent-learning activities will keep children occupied (and learning!)

✔ when they arrive early,

✔ when an individual or a group finishes an activity before the others, or

✔ when there is extra time after the lesson.

You'll find a Time Stuffer in the introduction to each module. After a quick setup, children can use the activity during all the lessons of the four- or five-week module.

You can also stretch your teaching time by doing one of the options you skipped earlier or by picking up one of the Bonus Ideas beginning on page 161.

● **You may want to write each lesson's outline and discussion questions on newsprint or a chalkboard.** This is a great way to prepare the lesson, and it will allow you to interact with the children instead of keeping your nose in the teachers guide. An added benefit is that children who read will have time to think about their answers.

● **Include time for Remembering God's Word.** These ideas, which are found in the introduction to each module, will help you teach a Bible verse to children. Fun, active memory-verse activities will help children hide God's Word in their hearts and apply it to their lives in a way that will really make a difference.

● **Rely on the Holy Spirit to help you.** Don't be afraid of children's questions. Remember, the best answers are those the children find themselves—not the ones teachers spoon-feed them.

# UNDERSTANDING YOUR FIRST- AND SECOND-GRADERS

## MENTAL DEVELOPMENT
- Interested in concrete learning experiences such as dramatizations and rhythms.
- Have a limited concept of time and space; are interested in the present but not in the past or future.
- Yearn for competence in developing skills.

## PHYSICAL DEVELOPMENT
- High energy levels demand a lot of physical activity such as jumping and running.
- Industrious; like to make things and complete projects.
- The finished product becomes more important than the process.
- Develop small-muscle coordination; begin to write.

## SOCIAL DEVELOPMENT
- Usually prefer to stick to same-sex friendships.
- Thrive on organized games and group activities.
- Want to please teachers but are beginning to recognize their role in relation to their peers.
- Want to win and always be first; have a strong sense of competition with others.

## EMOTIONAL DEVELOPMENT
- Express feelings with physical action.
- Crave individual attention and affirmation.
- Are self-centered; each child wants to be first.
- Feeling capable is directly related to self-esteem.
- Want everything to be fair; have a black-and-white sense of justice.

## SPIRITUAL DEVELOPMENT
- Understand God's love and God's world through personal experience.
- Don't comprehend the spiritual nature of God; think of God as a giant, a magician, or an invisible man.
- Don't comprehend the Bible's chronology except that the Old Testament came before Jesus and the New Testament talks about Jesus.
- Have a literal and concrete understanding of Bible stories and biblical truths; don't comprehend abstract ideas such as the Trinity.

# GROWING TOGETHER

Dear Parent,

I'm so glad to be your child's teacher this quarter. With our Hands-On Bible Curriculum™, your child will look at the Bible in a whole new way.

For the next 13 weeks we'll explore what Scripture has to say to first- and second-graders about Elijah, Ezra and Nehemiah, and school. Using active-learning methods and a surprising assortment of gadgets and gizmos (such as a rainbow shark, a bubble kit, and a spider web), we'll help children discover meaningful applications of God's Word.

Our Hands-On Bible Curriculum welcomes you to play an important part in what your child learns. Each week children will receive a "Growing Together" handout to take home and share. "Growing Together" features parenting tips, songs, crafts, prayers, and other activities to help you reinforce the Bible story and the point of each week's lesson.

Let me encourage you to use the "Growing Together" handout regularly; it's a great tool for promoting positive interaction and healthy communication in your family.

Sincerely,

# E·L·I·J·A·H

Elijah's story is as exciting as any other story in the Bible. A dynamic prophet, Elijah boldly spoke against the evil practices of King Ahab, who "did more things to make the Lord...angry than all the other kings before him" (1 Kings 16:33b). It didn't take long for Elijah to make enemies—Ahab referred to him as "the biggest troublemaker in Israel" (1 Kings 18:17b). Elijah's story climaxed when he faced 450 prophets of Baal in a test to see whether God or Baal was more powerful. Because Baal was a false god, made up by humans, Elijah and God won the contest easily, but Elijah quickly lost his courage and ran from the evil Queen Jezebel when she vowed to kill him.

It's easy to identify with Elijah. He knew that the true God was on his side, yet he was scared and uncertain—he felt alone in his struggle to follow God. But God reassured Elijah. Use these lessons to reassure the children in your class that God can be trusted to provide for them, to take care of the people they love, and to protect them when they're afraid. Your students will also learn that God is the only true God and that they can be confident because God is in control of the future. Have fun helping your class learn to rely on God in every situation.

## FIVE LESSONS ON ELIJAH

| LESSON | PAGE | THE POINT | THE BIBLE BASIS |
|---|---|---|---|
| 1—GOD PROVIDES | 17 | We can trust God to give us what we need. | 1 Kings 17:7-16 |
| 2—CARETAKER | 27 | God can take care of the people we love. | 1 Kings 17:17-24 |
| 3—NO CONTEST! | 37 | Our God is the only true God. | 1 Kings 18 |
| 4—FEAR NOT! | 47 | God protects us when we're afraid. | 1 Kings 19:1-18 |
| 5—IN HIS HANDS | 57 | God is in control of the future. | 2 Kings 2:1-14 |

# THE SIGNAL

During the lessons on Elijah, your attention-getting signal will be clapping your hands three times. Have children respond by clapping their hands three times as they stop talking and focus their attention on you. Tell children about this signal before the lesson begins. Explain that it's important to respond to this signal quickly so the class can do as many fun activities as possible.

# THE FIDGET BUSTER

When your students are too antsy to pay attention to the lesson, use this fidget buster to get the wiggles out.

Say: **Elijah was on the run a lot. Let's pretend we're running. Let's run to three places Elijah visited. When I say, "widow's house," sit down and pretend to eat as Elijah did when the widow shared bread with him. When I say "mountains," stand and fold your hands in prayer because Elijah prayed on the mountaintop. When I say "cave," kneel and cover your head to hide yourself as Elijah did when he ran away from the evil Queen Jezebel.**

Have the children stand and run in place. Randomly call out "widow's house," "mountains," or "cave." After children have completed the action that goes with each prompt, have them stand up and run in place until you prompt them again.

Play for several minutes, then say: **Then Elijah rested.** Have the children sit down to catch their breath as you return to your lesson.

# THE TIME STUFFER

The Time Stuffer for the five lessons on Elijah is a poster called "Elijah" found in the Learning Lab. The poster is a maze that will take children on a journey of Elijah's adventures. Along the way there are five ravens, 10 loaves of bread, five jugs of olive oil, 50 prophets, and 12 pitchers of water for the children to find.

When children arrive in class early or finish a project before others do, let them color the maze and keep track of the hidden items they find.

# REMEMBERING GOD'S WORD

Key verse: "The Lord is my strength and shield. I trust him, and he helps me. I am very happy, and I praise him with my song" (Psalm 28:7).

This module's key verse will help children learn to trust God. Use these activities any time during the lessons on Elijah.

## RESCUE ME!

Choose one child to be the jailer and one child to be the rescuer. Designate one corner of the room as the jail and another corner of the room as the safe place.

Say: **In this game, if you are tagged by the jailer, go to jail. If you are tagged by the rescuer, go to the safe place.**

Have the jailer and the rescuer close their eyes while everyone else hides. Tell the hidden children to shiver and shake and pretend to be afraid. When everyone is hidden, have the jailer and rescuer search for them. Give the rescuer a 10-second head start. Have the rescuer tap the children he or she finds and send them to the safe place. After 10 seconds, have the jailer look for the hidden children. If the jailer finds a child, the child must go to jail and continue to act scared.

After all of the children have been found by the jailer or the rescuer, end the game by clapping your hands three times. When the children have responded, gather them together and ask:

● **What did you think when the rescuer found you?** (I was glad; I was relieved.)

● **What did you think when the jailer found you?** (I was disappointed; I was mad.)

● **When do you feel like hiding in real life?** (When I get in trouble; during bad storms.)

● **When you're scared, what makes you feel better?** (To get a hug from my dad; to feel that God is with me.)

● **When do you feel safe and secure?** (When everything is going ok; when my family snuggles on the couch during a movie.)

Say: **All of us are scared sometimes. But God wants us to know that he's with us. Listen to what the Bible says.**

Read Psalm 28:7. Have the children repeat the verse after you.

Say: **God promises to be a shield that protects us from danger. God will rescue us when we're scared. We can trust God and be happy because God will keep his promise to be our shield.**

**The verse says that we can praise God with a song. Let's praise God by learning a song right now.**

Hang the "Lyrics Poster" from the Learning Lab at children's eye level. Listen to "You Are Lord" on the *cassette tape*. Then rewind the tape and have the children sing along. Have them sing the echo.

# SAFETY SHIELD

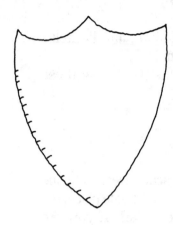

Before class, refer to the drawing in the margin to draw a shield on a piece of paper. Make enough photocopies of the shield to give each child one.

During class, read Psalm 28:7 to the children. Then ask:

● **What does God give us to help keep us safe?** (Parents; families; teachers; clothes; rules; friends; houses; nutritious food.)

If children have a hard time thinking of answers, get them started by mentioning a couple of the ideas above.

Write each idea on a separate shield. Then have each child use a glue stick to glue a shield to the cover of an old magazine. Ask:

● **What does God protect us from?** (Bad people; tornadoes; hurricanes.)

Have children brainstorm ideas until there are at least two ideas for each child. Write each idea on a separate sheet of old newspaper.

Have the children wad up the newspaper sheets, then stage a battle. Have half of the children throw the newspaper wads while the other children protect themselves with their magazine shields. When all the wads have been thrown, have the children switch roles—those who protected themselves will now become the attackers while those who threw newspaper wads will protect themselves with their magazine shields.

After the battles, clap your hands three times to get children's attention. When they've responded by clapping their hands three times, have them leave the shields and newspaper wads on one side of the room and sit on the floor with you on the other side of the room. Ask:

● **What did the shields do during the battles?** (They kept me from being hurt; the paper bounced off them.)

● **How has God been like a shield for you?** (God protects me from being hurt; God takes care of me.)

● **What would happen if you didn't have a shield during a battle?** (I might die; I'd get hurt.)

Say: **We can be happy because God promises to be our shield. Listen again to what the verse says.** Read Psalm 28:7 and have the children repeat it after you.

# G·O·D

# P·R·O·V·I·D·E·S

## THE POINT
We can trust God to give us what we need.

It's important to say The Point just as it's written in each activity. Repeating The Point over and over will help children remember it and apply it to their lives.

## THE BIBLE BASIS:
1 Kings 17:7-16. A widow shares her bread.

Elijah lived by trust and obedience. When God told him to hide from King Ahab in a ravine east of the Jordan river, Elijah obeyed. When God said he would send ravens with food and provide a stream to drink from in the middle of a drought, Elijah trusted God. When God told Elijah to ask a poor, starving widow for food, Elijah obeyed, knowing that God would provide what he needed and that God would take care of the widow and her son. God miraculously cared for them. Until the end of the drought, the widow's supply of oil and flour was never depleted.

God faithfully cared for Elijah, the widow, and her son. God promises to take care of us, too. Most American children have enough food and plenty of clothes to wear. Even so, children worry about who will take care of them if their parents divorce or die. And many of our nation's children *don't* have enough to eat or wear. This lesson will help your class see that God is taking care of them every day. They'll learn to rely on God and to turn to him for whatever they need.

Other Scriptures used in this lesson are Psalm 31:19; Matthew 7:9-11; and James 1:17.

## KEY VERSE
for Lessons 1–5

"The Lord is my strength and shield. I trust him, and he helps me. I am very happy, and I praise him with my song" (Psalm 28:7).

# GETTING THE POINT

Children will

● discover that God gives only good gifts,

● learn that they can trust God to provide for them, and

● find out that God has good things stored up for them.

Before the lesson, collect the items from the Learning Lab for the activities you plan to use. Refer to the pictures in the margin to see what each item looks like.

# THIS LESSON AT A GLANCE

| SECTION | MINUTES | WHAT CHILDREN WILL DO | LEARNING LAB SUPPLIES | CLASSROOM SUPPLIES |
|---------|---------|-----------------------|------------------------|---------------------|
| WELCOME TIME | up to 5 | **Welcome!**—Receive a warm welcome from the teacher and make name tags. | | "Trust God" name tags (p. 25), markers, scissors, tape |
| ATTENTION GRABBER | up to 10 | **Grab a Bug**—Grab as many black bugs as they can in 30 seconds and talk about greed, desires, and needs. | Jump-rope, black insects | |
| BIBLE EXPLORATION & APPLICATION | up to 13 | **Elijah and the Widow**—Learn from 1 Kings 17:7-16 of how God provided food for Elijah and a widow during a famine. | | Bible, popcorn, popcorn popper, large bowl, small measuring cup, vegetable oil |
| | up to 10 | **Bugs and Raisins**—Hunt for provisions and learn from Matthew 7:9-11 that God will provide good things for them just as their parents do. | Black insects | Bible, napkins, tape or stapler, raisins, peanuts, bowl, popcorn |
| | up to 12 | **Stored Up**—Feed bugs to a shark, read Psalm 31:19, and talk about the good gifts that God has stored up for them. | Black insects, rainbow shark | Bible |
| CLOSING | up to 10 | **Conducted Prayer**—Read James 1:17, think of things that God has provided, and thank God for those things with a fun prayer. | Tinsel wand | Bible |

Remember to make photocopies of the "Growing Together" handout (p. 26) to send home with your children. "Growing Together" is a valuable tool for helping first- and second-graders talk with their parents about what they're learning in class.

# T·H·E  L·E·S·S·O·N

##  ELCOME TIME

### WELCOME!

**(up to 5 minutes)**

- Greet each child individually with an enthusiastic smile.
- Thank each child for coming to class today.
- Say: **Today we're going to learn that**  **we can trust God to give us what we need.**
- Help children make name tags. Photocopy the "Trust God" name tags (p. 25) and follow the instructions.
- Tell the children that the attention-getting signal you'll use during this lesson is clapping your hands three times. Ask children to respond by clapping their hands three times as they stop talking and focus their attention on you. Rehearse the signal with the children, telling them to respond quickly so you have plenty of time for all the fun activities planned for this lesson.

**THE POINT** ★

## TTENTION GRABBER

### GRAB A BUG

**(up to 10 minutes)**

Form a circle on the floor with the *jump-rope*. Scatter all but four of the *black insects* inside the circle. You'll use the other four bugs in the "Bugs and Raisins" activity.

Choose a volunteer to go first. Give your volunteer 30 seconds to grab as many bugs as possible while remaining on the outside of the circle. The volunteer must hold all the bugs he or she has grabbed while grabbing more bugs.

At the end of 30 seconds, congratulate the volunteer and have him or her return the bugs to the circle. Choose another volunteer to play. Keep playing until each child has had a turn. Then return the *black insects* and the *jump-rope* to the Learning Lab. Gather the children in a circle and ask:

- **How many bugs did you grab?** (20; 30; 18.)
- **Were you satisfied with how many you got, or did you want more?**

**LEARNING LAB**

(I got more than anyone, so I was happy; I wasn't happy because I wanted all of them.)

● **In this game, it was fun to be greedy, to grab all that you could. What does it mean to be greedy in real life?** (It means wanting more than anyone else; it means wanting everything; it means not sharing.)

Say: **When we're greedy, we're not satisfied just to have what we need. We want to get more and more. Today we're going to talk about the opposite of being greedy—we're going to talk about the things that we really need and where they come from.** Ask:

● **What do we need in life?** (God; food; clothes; a place to live.)

Say: **Let's talk about a man, a woman, and a boy in the Bible who didn't have everything they needed. They learned, just as we'll learn, that ✦ we can trust God to give us what we need.**

 **THE POINT**

# BIBLE EXPLORATION & APPLICATION

## ELIJAH AND THE WIDOW 📖

### (up to 13 minutes)

Bring a popcorn popper to class so that you can pop popcorn at the end of this story. Measure enough raw popcorn to make a big bowl of popcorn. Put the raw popcorn in a small measuring cup. (Also bring oil if your popper calls for it.) If your popper needs to heat up before it can be used, plug it in before you begin the story. Keep children away from the popper so they don't get burned.

Have the children gather on the floor. Say: **I need your help with our story. There are three main characters: the widow, Elijah, and God. When I say, "the widow," rub your stomach to show that she was very hungry. When I say "Elijah," say, "a man of God" to show that he was a prophet. When I say "God," point to heaven. I have something else that will help tell the story.** Show children a small handful of the raw popcorn. **Listen to find out what can happen with a small amount of food.**

Open your Bible to 1 Kings 17:7-16. Say: **There had been no rain in the land of Israel for a long time. The ground dried up, the plants shriveled, and the people started to run out of food. They began to worry about having enough to eat.**

**Elijah** (pause) **was a prophet. God** (pause) **took care of him during the famine by sending birds with bits of bread and meat for him to eat. But**

one day, God (pause) **told Elijah** (pause) **to go to a widow's** (pause) **home and stay with her for a while.**

**Elijah** (pause) **obeyed and found the widow** (pause) **gathering sticks for a fire. He said, "Please, bring me some water to drink. I'm very thirsty." As she left to bring him a drink of water, he added, "And while you're getting me a drink, please bring me some bread to eat."**

**The widow** (pause) **said, "But I have no bread. I have only a little bit of flour and oil.** (Hold up the small cup of raw popcorn.) **It's only enough to make a small meal for my son and me, and then we will starve because there is no more food."**

**Elijah** (pause) **said, "Don't worry. Go home and bake the bread, then bring it to me to eat. Then go back and cook something for you and your son. God** (pause) **promises that you will never run out of flour or oil until it rains again."**

**The widow** (pause) **believed and went home to bake the bread.** (Pour the popcorn into the popper or bring out the bowl of popped popcorn.) **And from that day on, the flour and oil never ran out. The widow** (pause), **her son, and Elijah** (pause) **had plenty to eat. God** (pause) **kept his promise and took care of them.**

While the corn is popping, ask:

● **When have you felt really hungry?** (I'm hungry when I get home from school; once we went on a trip and left our lunches at home by mistake; sometimes I forget to eat breakfast.)

● **What do you do when you're hungry?** (I ask my mom for a snack; I rub my stomach; I try not to think about food.)

When the popcorn has finished popping, show it to the children. Save the popcorn for the next activity. Say: **Look how much popcorn there is! We'll enjoy it in a few minutes. This big bowl of popcorn was made from a few kernels. In the Bible story, God took a small amount of flour and oil and made it last for a long, long time.**

● **How did God keep the widow from running out of flour and oil?** (I don't know; it was a miracle; God can do anything he wants to.)

● **Why did the widow believe Elijah and share the little bit of food she had left?** (Because she knew he was from God; because she trusted him; because she trusted God.)

● **Elijah and the widow trusted God to provide food for them. What do you trust God for?** (Food; clothes; that my parents will take care of me.)

Say: ✖ **We can trust God to give us what we need. The widow and Elijah were very hungry, but they believed that God would keep providing for them even when they were almost out of food. God will do the same for us when we trust him completely. Let's find out more about God's promise to give us good things.**

# BIBLE INSIGHT

The widow of Zarephath thought she was preparing her last meal when she met Elijah. Her simple act of faith resulted in a miracle. Every miracle, large or small, begins with an act of obedience. We may not see the solution until we take that first step of faith.

## Teacher Tip

If you brought already-popped popcorn for this activity, put the bowl of popcorn in the center of the circle during this discussion.

**THE POINT**

# BUGS AND RAISINS 📖

## (up to 10 minutes)

Before class, prepare one of these small surprise pouches for each child in your class. Fold a paper napkin in half and tape or staple the sides together to create a small pouch. Put three or four raisins in most of the pouches. In no more than four of the pouches put one of the *black insects*. Then tape or staple the pouches shut. Hide the pouches around the room.

Also mix raisins and roasted peanuts in a bowl. Hide the mix where the children won't find it.

During class, have the students sit on the floor with you. Say: **For fun, I've hidden a special pouch for each person somewhere in the room.**

Have the children hunt until each child has found a pouch. Make sure that more than one child has a pouch with a bug in it. Have the children bring their unopened pouches back to the circle. Have each child open the pouch he or she has found and put its contents on top of the napkin. Then put the *black insects* back in the Learning Lab and fill each child's napkin with raisins, peanuts, and popcorn. As kids enjoy the snack, ask:

● **What did you think when you saw that some of the pouches had plastic bugs in them?** (I was surprised; I thought it was a dirty trick; I thought it was funny.)

● **Would you rather eat bugs or raisins? Explain.** (I'd rather eat raisins because bugs are icky; neither, because bugs aren't food and raisins taste bad; I'd rather have raisins because the bugs are plastic.)

Say: **Listen to what the Bible says about what we receive from God.** Read Matthew 7:9-11. Ask:

● **Why does God give us good gifts instead of bad gifts?** (Because God loves us; because he's God; because God promises to take care of us.)

Say: **When we ask God to take care of us, we can be sure that he will. God promises to bring us the good things that we need. Your parents would never give you stones to eat when you need bread, and God will never give us bad gifts.** ✦ **We can trust God to give us what we need; God will never let us down.**

★ **THE POINT**

# STORED UP 📖

## (up to 12 minutes)

Have the children sit in a circle. Put the *black insects* in the middle of the circle. Hold up the *rainbow shark* and say: **This is a very hungry shark. We need to find some food that he likes before he starts tasting our fingers. Let's see if he likes black bugs.** Put a bug in the shark's mouth and hold the shark vertically so the bug drops down into the shark's "stomach."

Say: **I think this shark likes bugs. Let's all take a turn feeding the shark. When you put a bug inside the shark, tell us something that you have every day that you're thankful for—something you need that God has provided.**

Pass the shark to your left and have the child pick up a bug, mention something he or she is thankful for, and put the bug inside the shark's mouth. Then have the child pass the shark to the next person. Continue until everyone has had a turn. If you'd like, continue until all the bugs are inside the shark. Then say: **This shark is full of good things that come from God. Listen to what the Bible says about what God has for us.** Read Psalm 31:19. Then ask:

● **What does it mean to store up goodness?** (It means that you save it; it means that you keep it ready.)

● **Why does God store up good things for us?** (Because we trust him; because God loves us.)

● **We've talked about the things that God has already given us. What do you think God has stored up for your future?** (A new bike; good breakfasts; good plans for my future.)

Say: **God has given us a lot of great things to eat, just as we've given lots of bugs to this shark to eat. This shark is full of good things that come from God. Our lives are full of good things, too, things such as . . .** (Mention some of the things the children talked about earlier.) ★ **We can trust God to give us what we need. We don't have to worry about being empty, because God has enough for everyone. Let's thank God for all the gifts he's given to us.**

Return the *rainbow shark* and *black insects* to the Learning Lab.

**THE POINT** ★

---

**W**e believe Christian education extends beyond the classroom into the home. **GROWING TOGETHER** Photocopy the "Growing Together" handout (p. 26) for this week and send it home with your children. Encourage children and parents to use the handout to plan meaningful activities on this week's topic. Follow up the "Growing Together" activities next week by asking children what their families did.

# CLOSING

## CONDUCTED PRAYER 📖

### (up to 10 minutes)

**LEARNING LAB**

Ask:
- **What did you learn today?** (I learned that God will give me what I need; I learned that God gives me good things; I learned that I can trust God to take care of me.)

Say: **Listen to what the Bible says about good gifts.** Read James 1:17. Ask:
- **Why does God give us good gifts?** (Because he loves us; because he takes care of us.)

Say: **Each of us is a special creation. God made each one of us and loves us so much that he promises to take care of us forever. Let's think about our gifts.**

Have children each think of one thing that God provides for them. They might think of general things such as life, clothes, homes, or food. Or they might think of specific things such as a new bicycle, a baby brother, or an A in math. Have each person say his or her idea aloud so you can make sure that each person has a different idea.

Then have the class stand in a circle. Stand in the center of the circle. Show the children the *tinsel wand*. Say: **This wand is my director's baton. I'm going to pretend that I'm an orchestra director. You will be my orchestra. The gift you have chosen will be your instrument. Each time I point my baton at you, call out the one thing you've chosen that God has provided for you. Then, when I point my baton straight up in the air, say,** ✦ **"We can trust God to give us what we need. Thank you, God!" Let's practice that.**

✦ **THE POINT**

✦ **THE POINT**

Point the *tinsel wand* straight up in the air and say with the children: ✦ **We can trust God to give us what we need. Thank you, God!**

Then randomly point the *tinsel wand* at different children. For fun, really ham it up and act like an orchestra conductor. You can point to children on opposite sides of the circle at the same time, point behind your back, point at the same child three or four times, and wave the wand at several children at the same time. You can indicate to one child to call out his idea softly and indicate to another child to call out her idea loudly. Periodically, point the wand in the air.

If you have time, let the children take turns being the conductor.

Then have everyone call out "amen."

# TRUST GOD

Photocopy this page and cut apart the name tags as indicated. Have children color their name tags and write their names on the lines.

**ELIJAH 1:**

We can trust God to give us what we need.

**KEY VERSE**

*"The Lord is my strength and shield. I trust him, and he helps me. I am very happy, and I praise him with my song"* (Psalm 28:7).

# GROWING TOGETHER

## I·N T·O·U·C·H

Today your child learned that every good gift comes from God. The children learned that God is trustworthy; when God says he'll provide good things for us, we can be sure that he will. The children discovered that God already has an abundance of gifts stored up and ready for them. Use these ideas this week to help your child learn that God will provide.

### BIRD-BATH

In Matthew 6, Jesus tells us to learn about trusting God by watching how God takes care of the birds. Create a sanctuary for the birds in your neighborhood this week. Place the lid of your garbage can upside down on top of the can so it creates a shallow basin. Line the lid with gravel or small rocks. Spell out "Don't worry" with the gravel. Fill the lid with one to two inches of water. Then watch as the birds bathe and preen.

### BREAKFAST GIFTS

Make your favorite pancake recipe. After you pour the batter into the skillet, sprinkle a spoonful of wheat germ or granola over the top of each pancake. When the pancakes have cooked on both sides, immediately drizzle them with honey and roll them up. As you eat the pancake rolls, read Psalm 81:16 and talk about the good gifts that God gives you.

### SURE AS THE SUNRISE

Rise with your family before dawn and snuggle together as you watch the sunrise. Sip hot chocolate and sing quiet praise songs together. Before the sun has risen, read this portion of Hosea 6:3: "Let's try to learn  about the Lord; he will come to us as surely as the dawn comes." After the sun has risen, read Isaiah 60:1 joyfully. Talk about how God is as trustworthy as the sunrise. If the day is cloudy, talk about how you know that God is with you even though you can't see him just as you know the sun is behind the clouds.

### GIFTS FOR ALL

Visit a pond, pool, lake, stream, or ocean near your home. Take a plastic cup and a bucket. See how many cupfuls of water it takes to fill the bucket. Then try to guess how many people could be given a cup of water from the body of water before it would dry up. (Be sure to caution your child not to drink the water.) Then read Philippians 4:19. Tell your child that the body of water is like God's riches. God has so much that his supply will never run out, and God wants to share these riches with us.

# C·A·R·E-
# T·A·K·E·R

It's important to say The Point just as it's written in each activity. Repeating The Point over and over will help children remember it and apply it to their lives.

## THE BIBLE BASIS:

1 Kings 17:17-24. Elijah raises the widow's son from the dead.

Elijah was staying with a widow who had only one son. He was the only family member left to her since her husband had died. After Elijah had been with them for a while, the son became very ill and finally stopped breathing. Then the widow was all alone, without a husband or children to care for. She turned on Elijah in anger. "Did you come here to remind me of my sin and to kill my son?" she asked. Elijah took the boy, placed him on a bed, and pleaded with God to restore his life. God heard Elijah's cry, and the boy came back to life. When the widow saw her son alive again, her faith was restored and strengthened.

Obviously, not everyone we care about is healed from sickness and disease. But every day, people narrowly avoid accidents, are victorious over illness, and survive natural disasters. God does take care of the people we love—even when he takes them to heaven to make them well. God cares about our loved ones more than we can imagine. Use this lesson to help children learn that they can trust God to take care of them and those around them. No matter what, God won't abandon us.

Other Scriptures used in this lesson are Psalm 3:3 and Psalm 147:4-5.

## KEY VERSE
### for Lessons 1–5

"The Lord is my strength and shield. I trust him, and he helps me. I am very happy, and I praise him with my song" (Psalm 28:7).

# GETTING THE POINT

Children will

- learn that God is their shield,
- discover that God has enough power to take care of everyone, and
- find that they can trust God to take care of themselves and their loved ones.

Before the lesson, collect the items from the Learning Lab for the activities you plan to use. Refer to the pictures in the margin to see what each item looks like.

# THIS LESSON AT A GLANCE

| SECTION | MINUTES | WHAT CHILDREN WILL DO | LEARNING LAB SUPPLIES | CLASSROOM SUPPLIES |
|---|---|---|---|---|
| WELCOME TIME | up to 5 | **Welcome!**—Receive a warm welcome from the teacher and make name tags. | | "Trust God" name tags (p. 25), markers, scissors, tape |
| ATTENTION GRABBER | up to 10 | **Rabbit**—Be chased by a hunter and talk about being worried about their safety and the safety of those they love. | Foam shapes | |
| BIBLE EXPLORATION & APPLICATION | up to 13 | **The Widow's Son**—Learn what happened when the widow's son died and discover that God will take care of them and their loved ones. | | Bible |
| | up to 10 | **Count the Bubbles**—Try to count a lot of soap bubbles and learn from Psalm 147:4-5 that God's power is greater than their own. | Bubble kit *recommend regular bubble liquid* | Bible, water |
| | up to 10 | **A Shield**—Form a human shield to protect the black bugs and learn from Psalm 3:3 that God is a shield around them and the people they love. | Black insects, foam shapes, plastic foam | Bible |
| CLOSING | up to 12 | **Family Shields**—Make shields around their families and sing a song thanking God for his protection. | | "Shield" handout (p. 35), paper or chalkboard and chalk, scissors, markers |

Remember to make photocopies of the "Growing Together" handout (p. 36) to send home with your children. "Growing Together" is a valuable tool for helping first- and second-graders talk with their parents about what they're learning in class.

## WELCOME TIME

### WELCOME!

**(up to 5 minutes)**

- Greet each child individually with an enthusiastic smile.
- Thank each child for coming to class today.
- As children arrive, ask them about last week's "Growing Together" discussion. Use questions such as "What did you do to learn about trusting God?" and "What did you discover about what God gives to us?"
- Say: **Today we're going to learn that** ⭐ **God can take care of the people we love.**
- Help children put on their name tags. If some children weren't in class last week, or if some of the name tags were damaged, photocopy the "Trust God" name tags (p. 25) and have children follow the instructions to create new name tags.
- Tell the children that the attention-getting signal you'll use during this lesson is clapping your hands three times. Ask children to respond by clapping their hands three times as they stop talking and focus their attention on you. Rehearse the signal with the children, telling them to respond quickly so you have plenty of time for all the fun activities planned for this lesson.

**THE POINT** ⭐

*God can take care of the people we love.*

## ATTENTION GRABBER

### RABBIT

**(up to 10 minutes)**

Choose one child to be the hunter. Divide the rest of the class into groups of three. In each trio, choose one child to be the rabbit. The other two children will face each other and join hands to form a rabbit hutch.

If your class can't be evenly divided by three, form as many groups of three as possible and have the extra children be rabbits.

The hunter will toss the *foam shapes* at the rabbits as the rabbits run from the hunter. The rabbits may hide in a hutch and be safe from the hunter, but

**LEARNING LAB**

**THE POINT**

they may only stay there for three seconds. No rabbit may seek safety in the same rabbit hutch twice in a row, unless you have a small class and there is only one hutch. If a rabbit is hit by one of the *foam shapes,* he or she becomes the hunter, the hunter becomes a rabbit, and the chase begins again.

The rabbit hutches may move around the room, too, looking for rabbits who are in danger of being hit and trying to reach the rabbits before they get hit.

Give the *foam shapes* to the hunter and say "go" to start the game.

Stop the game every now and then and have the rabbits trade places with children forming the rabbit hutches so that everyone has a chance to be chased.

After several minutes, end the game. Return the *foam shapes* to the Learning Lab, then gather the children on the floor and ask:

● **What did you think when you were being chased by the hunter? Were you scared, excited, or what?** (I was scared because I didn't want to be caught; I thought it was exciting to be chased; I thought it was fun and scary all at the same time.)

● **How did you feel while you were in the rabbit hutch?** (I felt safe; I was happy; I was glad to escape from the hunter.)

● **When do you get worried and scared about your safety in real life?** (When it's storming; when I hear about people shooting each other.)

● **When do you feel safe in real life?** (When my parents are around; when I'm tucked into bed; when I'm at church.)

Say: **We all worry about our safety and the safety of the people we care about. Today we're going to talk about a widow who was worried about her son. Something terrible happened to him. But she learned that ✦ God can take care of the people we love.**

# B IBLE EXPLORATION & APPLICATION

## THE WIDOW'S SON 📖

### (up to 13 minutes)

Say: **In today's story, a widow's son gets sick. Let me hear you cough as if you were sick** (pause). **Now let me hear your cough when it gets worse** (pause). **Good! You'll also need to count out loud to three. Let's do that. One! Two! Three! And you'll need to cheer** (pause).

Open your Bible to 1 Kings 17:17-24. Say: **Today our story is about Elijah, the widow we learned about last week, and her son.**

**Elijah stayed with the widow for a long time. One day the widow's son got sick.** (Have the children cough.) **He didn't feel well at all. And every day he got worse and worse.** (Have the children cough more and more.) **One day, he stopped breathing.** (Hold your finger on your lips and say "hush.") **The boy died.**

**The widow was very sad. Her husband had already died, and her son was the only family member left to her. She loved her son, and she felt terrible when he died. The widow said to Elijah, "Why has this happened? Why did you do this to me? Did you come to remind me of my sin and punish me by killing my son?"**

**Elijah felt bad, too. He took the boy and placed him on a bed. Then he prayed: "God, this kind widow has allowed me to stay in her home. She is taking care of me just as you asked. How could you let her son die? Lord God, please let this boy live again."**

**Then he stretched out over the boy three times.** (Have the class count to three.)

**God heard Elijah's prayer and made the boy start to breathe again. Elijah carried him downstairs to his mother and said, "See! Your son is alive!"** (Have everyone cheer.)

**Then the widow said, "Now I know that you are a man from God. God really does speak through you!"** Ask:

● **What's it like when you're sick?** (I feel awful; I have to stay indoors; I get to stay home from school.)

● **How do you feel when someone you love gets sick?** (Worried; mad; sad; upset; when my mom's sick, I feel hungry because there's no one to make dinner.)

● **Why did God answer Elijah's prayer?** (Because he loved the boy; because he cared about the widow.)

● **What would you have thought if you had seen the boy come back to life?** (I would have known that God had healed him; I'd be surprised to see a real miracle.)

● **Tell about a time you were worried because you were sick or because someone you knew was sick. What happened?** (My mom was really sick once, and the rest of us had to do all the cooking; my grandfather was in the hospital for an operation, but he's OK now; my uncle died in a car wreck.)

Say: **Being sick is no fun. And it can be scary when people we love are sick. Most of the time, people get better. But sometimes they stay sick for a long time, and they might even die, as the widow's son in our story did. It's hard to understand some things that happen. But we do know for sure that God loves all of his children. God promises that no matter what happens he'll take care of us. And we can trust that** ✸ **God can take care of the people we love, too.**

# BIBLE INSIGHT

## Teacher Tip

Be sensitive to kids who may be struggling with the death of family members, friends, or pets. Grief is tough for children. Some children are comforted by the idea that God sometimes takes people to heaven to make them well.

 **THE POINT**

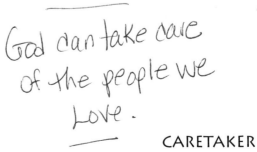
God can take care of the people we love.

# COUNT THE BUBBLES 📖

## (up to 10 minutes)

"The Lord is my strength and shield. I trust him, and he helps me. I am very happy, and I praise him with my song" (Psalm 28:7).

The widow had no hope left when her son died. She was angry—at God and at his servant Elijah. Yet God is all the hope we need because he promises to be a shield to protect us. When we focus our thoughts on God, our hope is restored.

 **THE POINT**

Before class, mix the bubble powder with water as directed on the *bubble kit* package. Let the mixture stand for at least 30 minutes before you use it. If you've already used the packet of bubble powder provided in the Learning Lab, mix two parts dish soap and one part water to make bubble water.

During class, have the children stand in a big circle. Say: **Each of us will have a chance to make bubbles. When it's your turn, dip the wand in the bubble water and wave the wand in the air. Then all of us will count all of the bubbles before they pop. I'll go first.**

Dip the perforated wand in the bubble water and wave it vigorously in the air. Have the children quickly count all of the bubbles they can. When all of the bubbles have popped, see how many bubbles the children counted. Then have the child on your right make bubbles.

Continue around the circle until everyone has had a chance to make bubbles. Then have the children sit down. Ask:

● **How many bubbles did you count? Could you count them all?** (25; 37; there's no way I could count them all before they popped.)

Say: **Sometimes we worry about the people we love, and we try to keep them safe and protected. When I blow these bubbles, try to keep them from popping.** Dip the wand in the bubble water one more time and wave it in the air. Have the children try to prevent the bubbles from popping. Set the *bubble kit* out of sight, then ask:

● **How did you feel when your bubble popped?** (Sad; disappointed; like I did a bad job.)

Say: **It's OK that we couldn't keep the bubbles from popping. We can't always keep the people we love safe, either. We're human beings. We're not like God; we don't have the power that he does. That's why we have to trust God. Listen to this Bible verse about God.** Read Psalm 147:4-5.

Say: **God could have counted all of the bubbles, and God could have kept them all from popping. We couldn't keep them safe, and we couldn't keep track of them all. But God can keep track of everything. He knows the name of every star, and he knows exactly how many hairs we have on our heads. God loves all of the people in the world, and ⭐ we can trust God to take care of the people we love. God covers us with protective love. Let's find out how it works.**

God can take care
of the people
we love.

# A SHIELD 📖

## (up to 10 minutes)

Scatter the *black insects* on top of a small table. Tear the *plastic foam* into smaller pieces. Distribute the pieces of *plastic foam* and the *foam shapes* to the children. Say: **Let's pretend that these foam pieces are bad things that happen to people.** Ask:

● **What bad things are you afraid might happen to the people you love?** (They might get in an accident; my parents might get divorced; my dad might move away; my grandma might die.)

Say: **Now let's try to knock the bugs off the table with the bad things.** Have the children stand around the table, about five feet away from it. Have them throw the *foam shapes* and *plastic foam* at the bugs. Give each child several tries.

Say: **If God didn't protect us, we might get hit by troubles like these bugs got hit with foam pieces.** Ask:

● **What does it feel like to have bad things happen to you?** (Scary; it feels like someone has beat me up; I just want to cry.)

Say: **Everyone gets hit by troubles sometimes. These bugs were scattered by the troubles that hit them. In the same way, we can feel like our whole lives have been messed up when troubles hit us. But God promises to protect us and the people we love. Listen to what the Bible says.** Read Psalm 3:3.

Have all the children stand in a circle around the table to shield the bugs. Gently toss the foam pieces at the bugs. It's OK if some of the foam pieces sneak through the shield. Gather the children and ask:

● **How do you feel, knowing that God promises to shield you?** (Good; happy; less worried.)

● **What do you think God will shield you and your family from?** (From getting sick; from dying; from being separated.)

Say: ✦ **God can take care of the people we love. God promises to take care of us, to protect us, and to be a shield for us. But bad things still happen sometimes. That's hard to understand. When God says he'll shield us, he doesn't mean we'll never get hurt. What God means is that even when we do get hurt, he'll be with us and love us and take care of us. We can trust God with the people we love because God promises to be with all of us and love all of us, all of the time.**

Return the *black insects, foam shapes,* and *plastic foam* to the Learning Lab.

---

### Teacher Tip

If there are kids in your class who are going through tough times, give them plenty of time to talk about what's happening in their lives. Take time to pray about their situations, asking God to care for them and everyone else involved.

---

**THE POINT** ✦

*God can take care of the people we love.*

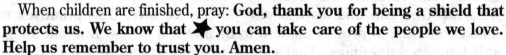

We believe Christian education extends beyond the classroom into the home. **GROWING TOGETHER** Photocopy the "Growing Together" handout (p. 36) for this week and send it home with your children. Encourage children and parents to use the handout to plan meaningful activities on this week's topic. Follow up the "Growing Together" activities next week by asking children what their families did.

#  CLOSING

## FAMILY SHIELDS

### (up to 12 minutes)

Before class, photocopy the "Shield" handout (p. 35) for each child.
During class, ask:

● **What did you learn today?** (I learned that God protects us; I learned that God loves us; I learned that God will be with me even when bad things happen.)

Give each child a photocopy of the "Shield" handout and have children cut on the solid lines. Show the children how to fold the handout on the dotted lines so that it looks like a shield. On the middle section, have them draw pictures of their families. Then have them fold their shields over the pictures. On the outside, have them write, "God is our shield." Print the words on a piece of paper or a chalkboard to help children with spelling.

 **THE POINT**

When children are finished, pray: **God, thank you for being a shield that protects us. We know that ✦ you can take care of the people we love. Help us remember to trust you. Amen.**

# SHIELD

Photocopy this handout for each child. Have the children cut out the shield then draw a picture of their families on the inside of the shield. Then have children fold the flaps and write "God is our shield" on the outside.

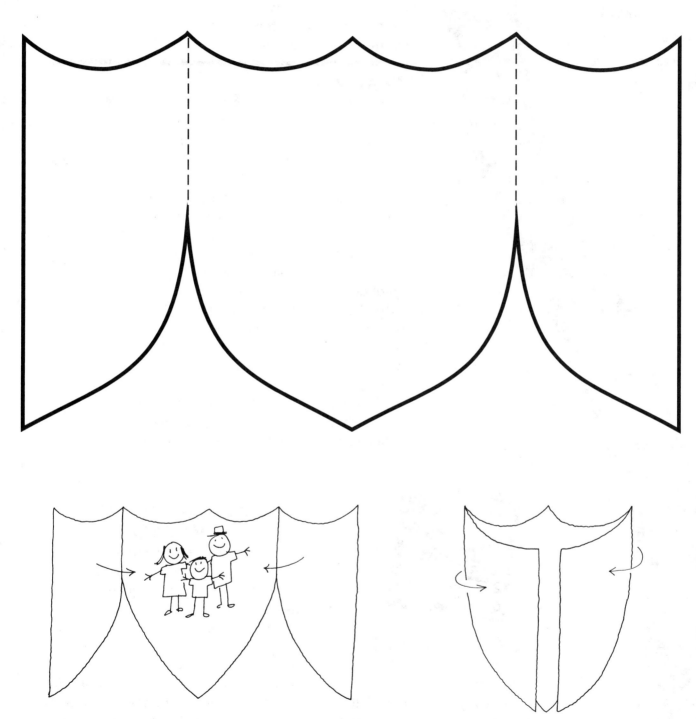

**ELIJAH 2:**

**God can take care of the people we love.**

### KEY VERSE

*"The Lord is my strength and shield. I trust him, and he helps me. I am very happy, and I praise him with my song"* *(Psalm 28:7).*

## GROWING TOGETHER

# I·N T·O·U·C·H

Today the first- and second-graders learned that no matter what happens, God can take care of them and the people they love. The children learned that God has amazing power and that he promises to care for them. The children also learned that God shields them from bad things and that even when bad things do happen, God is with them and loves them. Use these ideas to help children trust God's protection.

## SOUP MIX

Whip up this soup mix to give an under-the-weather friend. In a plastic bag, combine 4 teaspoons of chicken-broth mix or 4 chicken-broth cubes; 1 teaspoon of parsley flakes; ¾ cup of instant rice; and 1 teaspoon of dried, minced onion. Write these directions on a recipe card and place the card in the bag: "Boil 4 cups of water in a 2-quart pan, then stir in the contents of this package and wait (if you can!). While the pot bubbles and stews, remember that I am praying for you! P.S. You can enjoy the soup as soon as the rice is tender."

## GOD WATCHES

Sing this song together to the tune of "If You're Happy and You Know It":
God is watching over everyone I love.
God is reaching down his hand from above.
I can trust God for his care
'Cause God is everywhere.
God is watching over everyone I love.

## EMERGENCY

When the widow's son died, she knew to go to Elijah for help. Make sure that your child knows what to do and who to call in an emergency. Trim a 4×6 card with red ribbon. Write your local emergency numbers on it. Cut out photos of friends, neighbors, and nearby relatives. Glue the photos to the card and write their phone numbers next to their pictures. Post the card near your telephone. With your child, thank God for each person he uses to take care of those you love.

## GOOD-NIGHT VIDEO

Being separated from parents can make children anxious. When you must leave your child overnight, make a video to reassure your child. Read a bedtime story, say a prayer, and share one way that God will take care of you and your child while you're away. For example, you might say that God is providing a good time for you and has provided grandparents to take care of your child. When you return home, talk about how each of you felt God's care while you were separated.

# N·O
# C·O·N·T·E·S·T!

## THE POINT
Our God is the only true God.

It's important to say The Point just as it's written in each activity. Repeating The Point over and over will help children remember it and apply it to their lives.

## THE BIBLE BASIS:
1 Kings 18. Elijah and the prophets of Baal.

The stage was set for a major confrontation. King Ahab and the prophets of Baal had a monopoly on worship in Israel. The prophets of God had all been killed except for Elijah, Obadiah, and 100 prophets who were hidden away. Elijah confronted Ahab and called for a contest. Four hundred fifty prophets of Baal sacrificed a bull, put it on an altar piled with wood, and entreated their god to set fire to the wood. All day long the prophets prayed; they even engaged in self-mutilation to get the attention of Baal. Finally it was Elijah's turn. He built

an altar and piled it with wood and a sacrificed bull. Then he drenched the altar with 12 jars of water. He prayed a simple prayer and immediately the bull, the wood, the stones of the altar, and the water were consumed with fire. And the people learned that the God of Israel is the only true God.

The children in your class will love the drama of this story. And they'll love the completely one-sided victory that Elijah enjoyed. Use this lesson to help kids learn that God is just as powerful today as he was when he sent fire from heaven. Your students will also learn that the only God of the universe loves them and wants to develop a relationship with them that will last for eternity.

Other Scriptures used in this lesson are Deuteronomy 11:16; Psalm 8:3-4; Psalm 66; Psalm 95; Psalm 96; Psalm 98; and Psalm 148.

## KEY VERSE
for Lessons 1–5

"The Lord is my strength and shield. I trust him, and he helps me. I am very happy, and I praise him with my song" (Psalm 28:7).

# GETTING THE POINT

Children will

- learn that God is more powerful than any idol,
- see how false gods can distract them from following God, and
- find out that all of nature praises the one and only God.

Before the lesson, collect the items from the Learning Lab for the activities you plan to use. Refer to the pictures in the margin to see what each item looks like.

## THIS LESSON AT A GLANCE

| SECTION | MINUTES | WHAT CHILDREN WILL DO | LEARNING LAB SUPPLIES | CLASSROOM SUPPLIES |
|---|---|---|---|---|
| WELCOME TIME | up to 5 | **Welcome!**—Receive a warm welcome from the teacher and make name tags. | | "Trust God" name tags (p. 25), markers, scissors, tape |
| ATTENTION GRABBER | up to 10 | **Tug of War**—Play a variation of Tug of War until both sides are of equal strength, then learn that in the contest between God and Baal, all the power was on one side. | Jump-rope, lariat | Paper, marker, masking tape |
| BIBLE EXPLORATION & APPLICATION | up to 13 | **Elijah and the Prophets of Baal**—Listen to the story of Elijah and the prophets of Baal from 1 Kings 18 and discover how God proved that he is the one and only God. | Cassette: "Elijah and the Prophets of Baal," burlap | Bible, cassette player, book of matches, glass of water, paper cups |
| | up to 10 | **Distracted**—Play a game in which they are distracted from following the right person, hear Deuteronomy 11:16, and talk about the things that can distract them from the one and only God. | Visor, foam shape | Bible, paper, tape |
| | up to 12 | **Nature's Praise**—Participate in an action prayer from several psalms and learn that all of nature praises the only true God. | | Bible |
| CLOSING | up to 10 | **You Are Lord**—Learn from Psalm 8:3-4 that the only true God loves and cares for people, then sing a song about God's care. | Cassette: "You Are Lord," "Lyrics Poster" | Bible, cassette player |

Remember to make photocopies of the "Growing Together" handout (p. 45) to send home with your children. "Growing Together" is a valuable tool for helping first- and second-graders talk with their parents about what they're learning in class.

# T·H·E L·E·S·S·O·N

## WELCOME TIME

### WELCOME!

**(up to 5 minutes)**

● Greet each child individually with an enthusiastic smile.

● Thank each child for coming to class today.

● As children arrive, ask them about last week's "Growing Together" discussion. Use questions such as "What new song did you learn with your family?" and "What did you do to learn about God's protection?"

● Say: **Today we're going to learn that**  **our God is the only true God.**

● Help children put on their name tags. If some children weren't in class last week, or if some of the name tags were damaged, photocopy the "Trust God" name tags (p. 25) and have children follow the instructions to create new name tags.

● Tell the children that the attention-getting signal you'll use during this lesson is clapping your hands three times. Ask children to respond by clapping their hands three times as they stop talking and focus their attention on you. Rehearse the signal with the children, telling them to respond quickly so you have plenty of time for all the fun activities planned for this lesson.

**THE POINT** ★

## ATTENTION GRABBER

### TUG OF WAR

**(up to 10 minutes)**

Before class, draw a stick figure on a sheet of paper and write "Tug of War Champion" at the top of the paper. Also stick a 3-foot strip of masking tape to the middle of the floor.

Say: **We're going to play Tug of War with the *jump-rope*. But instead of seeing which side will win, we're going to work to make each side equally matched so that the *jump-rope* stays right in the middle.**

Loop the *lariat* around the midpoint of the *jump-rope* so the streamer will

**LEARNING LAB**

hang down over the masking tape line and indicate when the *jump-rope* is being tugged equally from both sides.

Form two teams and have them play Tug of War for about 15 seconds. Have the children pull on the rope, not on the handles. If one side is winning, move a player from the winning side to the losing side. Then have them tug again for 15 seconds. Keep moving children from team to team until both sides are evenly matched. Then ask:

● **Who will win a Tug of War contest between two equal sides?** (No one will; both teams will win.)

Have all the children join together to form one team and have them grab the rope. Tape the stick figure you drew earlier to the other end of the rope and say: **I'm really proud of the Tug of War champion that I've made. I'm certain that my champion will beat you.** Ask:

● **What do you think of my champion? Will he be able to beat you at Tug of War? Why not?** (He's just a piece of paper; he doesn't have any muscles; he won't be able to beat us.)

After the children have pulled the "champion" across the line, have them sit down. Put away the *jump-rope* and *lariat* and say: **Today's story is about a contest between the God of Israel and a false god named Baal that the king worshiped. Now we all know that ★ our God is the only true God. So we already know who won the contest. Baal was a made-up god just as my Tug of War champion is made up. My champion is just a piece of paper; he has no strength. Baal didn't have strength either. Let's find out how God showed that he is the only true God.**

 **THE POINT**

# B IBLE EXPLORATION & APPLICATION

## ELIJAH AND THE PROPHETS OF BAAL 📖

### (up to 13 minutes)

 **LEARNING LAB**

Cue the *cassette tape* to "Elijah and the Prophets of Baal." Also gather a book of matches and a glass of water. Place the *burlap* on the floor and surround it with empty paper cups. Make sure there's an empty cup for each child.

Gather the children around the *burlap,* open your Bible to 1 Kings 18, and say: **This exciting story comes from 1 Kings 18. Listen carefully because the tape will give you instructions. When you hear cheers, let out a cheer. When you hear a raspberry sound, say "boo." Also listen carefully so you'll know what to do with the cups that you see in the middle of our circle. Now let's listen to the story.**

Start the tape and listen to the story. When there are cheering sounds, encourage the children to cheer. When you hear a raspberry sound, encourage them to boo.

Also listen for the point in the story when water is poured over the altar. At that point you'll be told to stop the tape. Tell the children to pretend to pour water from the paper cups onto the *burlap* three times.

After the children have poured make-believe water on the *burlap,* say: **Let's do an experiment so we understand what happens in the story.**

Light one of the matches and let it burn for a few seconds, then blow it out. Say: **When a match is dry, it burns easily. But look what happens when it gets wet.**

Dip a new match in the glass of water, hold it there for a couple of seconds, and then try to light it. It won't light.

Say: **When matches and wood get wet, it's hard to set them on fire. But Elijah poured 12 jars of water on the altar before he prayed to God. Let's find out what happened.**

Turn the tape on again and listen to the end of the story. Then turn off the tape and ask:

● **Were you surprised at the ending? Why or why not?** (No, I knew God would win; I was surprised that so much stuff caught on fire.)

● **Why didn't anything happen when the 450 prophets prayed to Baal?** (Because their god wasn't real; because their god didn't have any power.)

● **Why do you think Elijah poured water on the altar?** (To show how much power our God has; to prove that our God is better.)

Say: **The prophets of Baal lost the contest before it even began. They prayed to statues that they had made themselves. There's no way that a statue can do anything; it's just a piece of wood or metal or clay or stone. Baal was a fake, and ★ our God is the only true God. God is greater than we are because he created us and the whole world. Elijah knew that, so he was sure he would win the contest.**

**King Ahab and the prophets of Baal had forgotten all about the true God when they made their own god to worship. Let's find out how they could have forgotten about God.**

Return the *burlap* to the Learning Lab.

# BIBLE INSIGHT

Although the prophets of Baal raved all afternoon, there was no reply—their "gods" were made of wood and stone. Today's secular gods—power, appearance, and possessions—are just as false and dangerous. They cause people to depend on something other than God, and when people call out to these gods, there is only silence. Only the true God can offer true answers, guidance, and wisdom.

**THE POINT**

# DISTRACTED 📖

## (up to 10 minutes)

Tape two sheets of paper to the sides of the *visor* to act as blinders. Experiment to create a very limited range of vision. With the *visor* on, you should be able to see only what is directly in front of you.

Choose a child to be the first to wear the *visor.* Say to the child with the *visor:* **Your job is to find out which person in the room is your partner and to follow him or her around the room. The way you'll identify your partner is that he or she will have a *foam shape* taped to his or her shirt.**

**LEARNING LAB**

## KEY VERSE Connection

"The Lord is my strength and shield. I trust him, and he helps me. I am very happy, and I praise him with my song" (Psalm 28:7).

Just as God flashed fire from heaven for Elijah, he will help us accomplish what he commands us to do. The proof may not be as dramatic in our lives as in Elijah's, but we can have faith that the only true God will provide what we need. God will give us the wisdom to raise a family, the courage to take a stand for truth, or the means to provide help for someone in need.

 **THE POINT**

Send the person wearing the *visor* out of the room while you tape a *foam shape* to the back of another child's shirt. Tell all of the children in the room that their job is to try to convince the person wearing the *visor* that they have a *foam shape* on their shirts. They can do anything they want to convince the person wearing the *visor* that they're his or her partner. Mention to the false partners that if they stand to the side of the person wearing the *visor,* he or she won't be able to see their shirts and it'll be easier to lead him or her astray.

Bring the person wearing the *visor* into the room and begin the game. Say to the person wearing the *visor:* **Listen to your classmates and decide which one to follow to the other end of the room. If you think you've chosen the wrong person, you can choose again.**

Play the game for a minute or two, then reveal who had the *foam shape.* Then choose another person to wear the *visor* and another person to be the true partner and play again.

Play several times as time allows, then put away the *foam shape* and the *visor.* Ask the children who wore the *visor:*

● **Why did you follow the people you followed?** (I followed Tina because she's my friend; I followed Dennis because he talked the loudest; I followed Tom because he showed me the *foam shape* on his back.)

● **How did you decide who was telling the truth?** (I looked for the *foam shape;* I listened for who was the loudest; I followed my friends.)

● **Did it make a difference if you could see the people who were trying to persuade you that they were your partners? Why or why not?** (Yes, because I saw the *foam shape;* no, because I couldn't see anyone's back.)

Say: **The false partners in this game tried to distract the person wearing the *visor* from finding the true partner. That's how it works with false gods. Listen to what the Bible says.** Read Deuteronomy 11:16. **False gods can fool us; they can distract us from God. A false god can be anything that keeps us from honoring God. For example, some people might care more about getting a lot of money than they do about obeying God.** Ask:

● **What are some other false gods, other things that people might care about more than they care about God?** (Having fun; toys; friends.)

Say: **It's OK to like money and toys and friends. Everything good that we have is a gift from God, and we can be thankful for it all. But sometimes people start to care more about things than they do about God. Then it's easy to be distracted from God. But ✦ our God is the only true God. And God wants us to be loyal to him. It's important to put aside all the things that distract us from God.**

# NATURE'S PRAISE 📖

## (up to 12 minutes)

Say: **Some people don't worship God. They don't understand that** ✦ **our God is the only true God. Some people choose to worship idols. Some people choose not to worship anything at all. But the Bible says that nature worships and praises God. Let's worship God the way nature does.**

THE POINT ✦

This praise prayer is based on verses from Psalm 66; Psalm 95; Psalm 96; Psalm 98; and Psalm 148.

Read aloud the following praise prayer and have the children do the actions indicated in parentheses. You may want to have a child who can read well or an adult helper lead the actions.

**Everything on earth, shout with joy to God!**
**All the earth worships God and sings praises to him.**
**Let the dolphins and the whales and the fish all praise God.**
*(Make dolphin, whale, and fish swimming motions.)*

**Let the rivers clap their hands in praise.** *(Clap loudly.)*

**Let the trees wave their branches in praise.** *(Wave your arms.)*

**Let the mountains sing for joy.** *(Raise hands over head and touch fingers to create a mountain shape. Shout, "Tum, ta dum," like a trumpet fanfare.)*

**Let sun, moon, and shining stars praise him—let everything in the sky praise God.**
*(Make a big circle with your arms for the sun, a smaller circle for the moon, and flick your fingers in the air for shining stars.)*

**Praise God from the earth. Let the birds of the air praise God.**
*(Flap arms and make bird noises.)*

**Let the beasts of the field—bears, tigers, and lions; sheep, cattle, and pigs; dogs, cats, and rabbits—all praise God together.** *(Make animal noises.)*

**Praise the Lord because he alone is great. He is more wonderful than heaven and earth.**
**Come, let's worship him and bow down.** *(Kneel.)*

**Let's kneel before the Lord who made us, because he is our God and we are the people he takes care of. Amen.**

After you've finished the prayer, have the children sit down. Ask:
● **Why does nature praise God?** (Because nature knows that God is powerful; because nature was created by God.)
● **What can humans do to praise God?** (Sing; pray; tell others about God; follow God's rules.)

Say: **Choose one thing that you can do to praise God this week. Then tell at least three people what you will do.**

Give children a minute to exchange ideas. Then have volunteers tell the class what they'll do to praise God during the week. Children might invite a neighbor to church, obey their parents promptly, or sing a praise song every night before bed.

Say: **When we praise God, we're telling him and the whole world that we know that ✦ our God is the only true God. Let's talk about another reason we can praise God.**

## ✦ THE POINT

**W**e believe Christian education extends beyond the classroom into the home. Photocopy the "Growing Together" handout (p. 45) for this week and send it home with your children. Encourage children and parents to use the handout to plan meaningful activities on this week's topic. Follow up the "Growing Together" activities next week by asking children what their families did.

# **C** LOSING

## YOU ARE LORD 📖

**(up to 10 minutes)**

Ask:

● **What did you learn today?** (I learned that God is the only God; I learned that God has more power than anyone else; I learned that nature praises God.)

Say: **Listen to this Bible verse. It asks a question. See if you know the answer.** Read Psalm 8:3-4 from the New Century Version: **"I look at your heavens, which you made with your fingers. I see the moon and stars, which you created. But why are people important to you? Why do you take care of human beings?"** Ask:

● **Do you know the answer? Why does God take care of people?** (Because God loves people; because God made people.)

## ✦ THE POINT

Say: **We can feel special because ✦ our God is the only true God and he loves each one of us. Let's sing a song to God to thank him for taking care of us.**

Sing "You Are Lord" with the *cassette tape.* Point to the words on the "Lyrics Poster" as you sing. At the end of the song, have all the children shout "amen" together.

Permission to photocopy this handout from Group's Hands-On Bible Curriculum™ for Grades 1 and 2 granted for local church use. Copyright © Group Publishing, Inc., P.O. Box 481, Loveland, CO 80539.

# GROWING TOGETHER

**ELIJAH 3:**
Our God is the only true God.

## KEY VERSE

*"The Lord is my strength and shield. I trust him, and he helps me. I am very happy, and I praise him with my song"* (Psalm 28:7).

## I·N T·O·U·C·H

Today your child learned that false gods and idols will never be able to compete with God because God is more powerful than anything or anyone else. The children also learned that a false god is anything that distracts them from honoring God. Use these ideas at home to help your child worship the one and only true God.

### GOD IS GREAT

This week, look all around you for evidence of God's greatness. Keep a piece of paper on your dining table and, before each evening meal, write down what you've seen. You might see God's power in a thunderstorm, God's sense of beauty in the delicate colors of wildflowers, or God's protection in the den of a woodland creature. Notice the multitude of stars, the warmth of the sun, and the sweet smell of the earth and air. Then thank God for being the only true God.

### FIRE POWER

Go to a local park for a picnic. Take along hot dogs to roast. If possible, collect fallen twigs and branches to make a fire. Take newspaper to help start the fire. Help your child arrange the wood and newspaper in

a fire pit. Light the fire yourself. Have your child stand nearby to help blow on the flames. Talk about how much work it takes to make a fire. Then read 1 Kings 18:30-38 and praise God for his power.

### RAIN PICTURES

Make a rain picture as a reminder that the one true God ended Israel's drought. Color a white sheet of paper with watercolor markers. Set it in the rain for a few seconds, then carefully carry it inside to dry. If you live in an area that doesn't get much rain, dip a toothbrush in water and run your fingers across the bristles, sending a fine spray of water onto your marker-colored paper.

### RISING TO THE TOP

Pour ½ cup of water into a large jar. Add 6 drops of food coloring and stir. Pour in ¼ cup of cooking oil. Then screw on the lid and shake the jar for 20 seconds. Watch as the oil separates from the water and rises. Talk about how God is the only God—God will always rise to the top in a competition between him and man-made gods. And just as the oil wouldn't stay mixed with the water, we can't worship God *and* man-made gods.

# F·E·A·R N·O·T!

## THE POINT
God protects us when we're afraid.

It's important to say The Point just as it's written in each activity. Repeating The Point over and over will help children remember it and apply it to their lives.

## THE BIBLE BASIS:
1 Kings 19:1-18. Elijah runs away.

Even after Elijah faced the king and 450 prophets of Baal alone and won, he was afraid when he knew that Jezebel, the queen, was after him. He ran for his life, and then, feeling like a failure, he asked God to let him die. But God wasn't finished with Elijah. God sent an angel with food and drink to strengthen Elijah. Then Elijah journeyed to Mount Sinai where he hid in a cave and told God about his troubles. God told Elijah to wait until he passed by. A strong wind rushed by, an earthquake shook the ground, and a fire blazed, but God wasn't in any of those things. When Elijah heard a gentle, quiet sound, he went out to meet with God.

Your students all feel afraid sometimes. And they're approaching the age at which they think they shouldn't be afraid. It's embarrassing to admit they're still afraid of the dark at the ripe old age of 7. It's good for children to learn that Elijah was scared even though he knew how powerful God was and that God was on his side. And God cared enough about Elijah to reassure him. Use this lesson to help children learn that God is always there, even when they're scared.

Other Scriptures used in this lesson are Psalm 91:2-6 and 1 Peter 5:7.

## KEY VERSE
for Lessons 1–5

"The Lord is my strength and shield. I trust him, and he helps me. I am very happy, and I praise him with my song" (Psalm 28:7).

# GETTING THE POINT

Children will

- talk about what scares them,
- see that God's protection is like a shield, and
- learn that they can cast their cares on God.

---

Before the lesson, collect the items from the Learning Lab for the activities you plan to use. Refer to the pictures in the margin to see what each item looks like.

## THIS LESSON AT A GLANCE

| SECTION | MINUTES | WHAT CHILDREN WILL DO | LEARNING LAB SUPPLIES | CLASSROOM SUPPLIES |
|---|---|---|---|---|
| WELCOME TIME | up to 5 | **Welcome!**—Receive a warm welcome from the teacher and make name tags. | | "Trust God" name tags (p. 25), markers, scissors, tape |
| ATTENTION GRABBER | up to 10 | **Scary Shark**—Play Scary Shark and talk about what they're afraid of. | Rainbow shark | |
| BIBLE EXPLORATION & APPLICATION | up to 13 | **Elijah Is Scared**—Listen to the story from 1 Kings 19 of Elijah's flight from Jezebel and learn that God is gentle with them when they're afraid. | Cassette: "Elijah Is Scared" | Bible, cassette player |
| | up to 10 | **Trapped**—Catch plastic bugs in a spider web and talk about the things that make people feel trapped, then read Psalm 91:2-6 and learn that God will rescue them. | Black insects, spider web | Bible, scissors |
| | up to 12 | **Cast Your Cares**—Create shapes representing their worries and fears, read 1 Peter 5:7, and toss their worries into the trash. | | Bible, paper, trash can |
| CLOSING | up to 10 | **God's Shield**—Sing about God's protection, then twirl a lariat above their heads and think about God's shield of protection around them. | Cassette: "You Are Lord," "Lyrics Poster," lariat | Cassette player |

Remember to make photocopies of the "Growing Together" handout (p. 55) to send home with your children. "Growing Together" is a valuable tool for helping first- and second-graders talk with their parents about what they're learning in class.

# T·H·E  L·E·S·S·O·N

## ELCOME TIME

### WELCOME!

**(up to 5 minutes)**

- Greet each child individually with an enthusiastic smile.
- Thank each child for coming to class today.
- As children arrive, ask them about last week's "Growing Together" discussion. Use questions such as "What did you learn about God's power?" and "What did you learn about the difference between God and idols?"
- Say: **Today we're going to learn that** ✦ **God protects us when we're afraid.**
- Help children put on their name tags. If some children weren't in class last week, or if some of the name tags were damaged, photocopy the "Trust God" name tags (p. 25) and have children follow the instructions to create new name tags.
- Tell the children that the attention-getting signal you'll use during this lesson is clapping your hands three times. Ask children to respond by clapping their hands three times as they stop talking and focus their attention on you. Rehearse the signal with the children, telling them to respond quickly so you have plenty of time for all the fun activities planned for this lesson.

**THE POINT** ✦

## TTENTION GRABBER

### SCARY SHARK

**(up to 10 minutes)**

Have the children sit in a circle. Hold up the *rainbow shark* and say: **Sharks are scary creatures. Let's talk about what we're scared of. I'll pass around the shark. When it comes to you, say one thing that you're scared of. I'll start. I'm scared of . . .** (Complete the sentence by naming something you're afraid of.)

When all the children have had a turn, have the children stand up. Say: **Let's play Scary Shark. We'll toss the shark around. When it comes to you,**

**LEARNING LAB**

pretend it's something you're scared of and quickly toss it to someone else.

Play Scary Shark for a few minutes. Then put the shark in the Learning Lab and have the children sit down again. Ask:

● **Why did you want to get rid of the scary shark so quickly?** (Because I don't like scary things; because it might have bitten me; I don't like to be afraid.)

● **What do you do when you're scared?** (I hide under the blankets; I find my mom or dad; sometimes I cry.)

● **Who or what protects you when you're afraid?** (God; our house protects me from storms; my teachers; my friends; my parents; the police.)

Say: **Everyone has fears. When we're afraid, sometimes we want to hide. Other times we may want to turn and run away. Today we're going to talk about a time when Elijah was scared. Even though Elijah knew that**  **God protects us when we're afraid, he was still scared. Let's find out what he did.**

# BIBLE EXPLORATION & APPLICATION

## ELIJAH IS SCARED

### (up to 13 minutes)

Cue the *cassette tape* to "Elijah Is Scared." This segment includes the sounds Elijah heard when he was in the cave on Mount Sinai. The story will tell you when to start and stop the tape.

Push several classroom tables together to represent the cave Elijah hid in.

Gather the children across the room from the tables. Show the children the story in 1 Kings 19:1-18. Have them follow you as you do the actions in this story.

Say: **King Ahab's wife was Queen Jezebel. She hated Elijah. She sent him a message that said, "By tomorrow I will have you killed."**

**When Elijah heard the message, he was so scared that he ran for his life.** (Slap your thighs with your hands to make running noises.)

**He ran and ran through the town of Beersheba and out into the desert. Finally he was tired, and he sat down under a bush. He wanted to give up. He was scared. He was hot and tired. He just wanted to die.**

**Elijah lay down under a tree and went to sleep.** (Make snoring noises.)

**Then an angel came and touched him. "Wake up, Elijah," the angel said. "I have brought you bread to eat and water to drink."**

**Elijah woke up and ate the food and drank the water. Then he went back to sleep.** (Make snoring noises.)

Later, the angel came again and brought more food. Elijah ate and drank and started on a long journey. He walked 40 days and 40 nights until he came to Mount Sinai, the mountain of God.

Elijah hid himself in a cave and stayed there all night. (Have the children sit underneath the tables and pretend they're in a cave.)

Then God said, "Elijah! Why are you here?"

Elijah answered, "All-powerful God, I have served you as well as I could. But the people have broken their agreement with you. I am the only prophet left, and they're trying to kill me. I'm scared."

God said, "Go, stand on the mountain, and I will pass by you."

Listen to the tape and be ready to tell me what Elijah heard.

Start the tape. There will be a loud, rushing wind sound. After the wind dies down, stop the tape and ask:

● **What did Elijah hear?** (Wind.)

Say: **But God wasn't in the ferocious wind.**

Start the tape and listen to the earthquake sounds. Then stop the tape and ask:

● **What did Elijah hear?** (Crashing; loud noises; something being broken.)

Say: **A tremendous earthquake shook the mountain and made huge rocks break in half. But God wasn't in the mighty earthquake.**

Start the tape and listen to fire noises. Then stop the tape and ask:

● **What did Elijah hear?** (A fire.)

Say: **It was a terrible fire, and God wasn't in the fire.**

Start the tape and listen to the gentle whisper. Stop the tape and ask:

● **What did Elijah hear?** (A gentle breeze; a whisper.)

Say: **Elijah heard a quiet, gentle sound. He knew that God was there, and he put his cloak around his face and went out to meet with God.** (Have the children leave the "cave.")

Then a voice said, "Elijah! Why are you here?"

And Elijah said again, "All-powerful God, I have always served you as well as I could. But your people have broken their agreement with you. All the prophets have been killed, and now the people want to kill me, too."

God said, "Don't worry. You're not alone. I have more for you to do. I want to help you choose a new and better king. And I want you to go and pour oil on Elisha as a sign that he will take over for you when you come to live with me. I'm taking care of all who have been faithful to me. There are 7,000 people in Israel who are still faithful to me.

Ask:

● **What was Elijah afraid of?** (He was afraid of the queen who wanted to kill him; he was afraid of dying; he was scared of being all alone.)

● **If you had been there when God sent wind, an earthquake, and a fire, what would you have done or thought?** (I would have been scared; I would have prayed for God to take care of me; I would've hidden in the cave.)

● **What did God sound like?** (God was quiet; like a whisper.)

# BIBLE INSIGHT

Elijah experienced the depths of discouragement just after his two great spiritual victories—the defeat of the prophets of Baal and the answered prayer for rain. God first let Elijah rest and eat, then he confronted him with the need to return to the work he had been given as God's prophet. God's purpose for Elijah's life was not yet over.

## THE POINT

● **What did God do to take care of Elijah?** (God kept him safe in the cave; God kept him from being killed; God sent an angel with food.)

Say: **Even when Elijah was scared, God was with him.** ✦ **God protects us when we're afraid. When Elijah was scared, God was quiet and gentle so that Elijah would feel safe. God wants us to feel safe, too. God loves you and will always take care of you, just as he took care of Elijah.**

# TRAPPED 📖

## (up to 10 minutes)

Have the children sit in a tight circle. Hold up the *spider web* and say: **This *spider web* isn't real.** Ask:

● **What does a spider have a web for?** (A web is a spider's house; spiders catch their food in their webs.)

Say: **One reason a spider has a web is to catch bugs to eat. Once a bug is trapped in a spider's web, getting away is almost impossible. The Bible tells about people getting caught in traps, too. People aren't eaten like bugs caught in a spider's web, but it can still be scary to be caught in a trap. Let's talk about the kinds of things that trap people. For instance, you might get trapped when someone pressures you to do something wrong. That can be scary because you can't see any way out.**

**For each trap we think of, we'll trap a *black insect* in this fake *spider web*.** Ask:

● **What can a person feel trapped by?** (By a temptation; by doing wrong; by telling lies.)

If children have a tough time thinking of ideas, mention the following traps: People might be trapped by their own temptations, by being afraid, by sins such as lying or disobeying, or by scary events such as floods and tornadoes.

As a child mentions an idea, have him or her put a *black insect* in the middle of the *spider web*.

Say: **When you feel trapped, you think you can't escape. When someone is pressuring you to do wrong, you may think you don't have any choice but to do wrong.**

Have the children gently grab the web and stretch it across the middle of the circle. Then have them gently try to untangle the bugs. (It'll be difficult.) Ask:

● **How did you feel as you tried to get the bugs out of the web?** (Upset because I couldn't do it; frustrated.)

● **How is that like the way you feel when you're trapped by a trouble?** (When I'm in trouble I think that no matter what I do I'll still be in trouble; I think that if I work on my problems they might just get worse.)

Say: **When we're trapped, we feel scared because we need help to get** out. **Listen to what the Bible says about God's help with traps and fears.** Read Psalm 91:2-6. Ask:

● **What will God do when we're scared?** (God will save us; God will rescue us; God will protect us.)

● **What will God do when we need his protection?** (God will hide us under his wings; protect us with his shield.)

Using scissors, clip the *black insects* out of the *spider web*. Have the children help.

Say: **No matter what kind of trouble we get into and no matter what we're afraid of, we can trust God to help us.** ✦ **God protects us when we're afraid. And God promises to rescue us from the traps we face.**

Return the *spider web* and *black insects* to the Learning Lab.

**THE POINT**

# CAST YOUR CARES 📖

## (up to 12 minutes)

Give each child a sheet of paper. Say: **Tear your sheet of paper into a shape that reminds you of something you're worried about or scared of.**

Give children two or three minutes to tear their papers. While they're tearing, have them brainstorm things that people worry about or are scared of. You don't need to write them down.

When the children are finished, have them stand in a circle. Put a trash can in the middle of the circle. Read 1 Peter 5:7. Ask:

● **What should we do with our worries and fears?** (Tell God about them; give them to God.)

Have the kids wad up the papers representing their worries and fears and toss them into the trash can. If some of the papers don't land in the trash can on the first throw, have the children pick them up and try again. Ask:

● **What happens to something once you've put it in the trash?** (It gets taken to the dump; it goes away.)

Say: **When we give our worries and fears to God, it's like throwing them away. God will take care of everything we're worried about or scared of.** ✦ **God protects us when we're afraid. Once we tell God about something, we don't have to think about it anymore. Let's thank God for his protection.**

**K**EY **VERSE** Connection

"The Lord is my strength and shield. I trust him, and he helps me. I am very happy, and I praise him with my song" (Psalm 28:7).

Elijah felt alone and afraid when Jezebel came after him and he was running for his life. Elijah was not alone. We are never as alone as we may feel; God is always with us.

**THE POINT**

**W**e believe Christian education extends beyond the classroom into the home. Photocopy the "Growing Together" handout (p. 55) for this week and send it home with your children. Encourage children and parents to use the handout to plan meaningful activities on this week's topic. Follow up the "Growing Together" activities next week by asking children what their families did.

**GROWING TOGETHER**

# CLOSING

## GOD'S SHIELD

### (up to 10 minutes)

Ask:

● **What did you learn today?** (I learned that God will help me when I'm scared; I learned that God will rescue me; I learned that I should tell God all about my worries because he cares about me.)

Together, sing "You Are Lord" with the *cassette tape*. Point to the words on the "Lyrics Poster" as you sing.

Then show the children how the *lariat* works. Hold it by the string, not by the plastic ribbon, and twirl it quickly above your head. If you don't hold it high enough or twirl it fast enough, you may end up tangled in the ribbon, so practice before class. You may want to reinforce the *lariat* by taping the string to the plastic piece.

**★ THE POINT**

Say: We know that ★ **God protects us when we're afraid. Let's pretend that this *lariat* is the shield around us that God provides. We're safe inside the ribbon.**

Have each child take a turn spinning the *lariat* above his or her head. Have the other children stand as far away as possible from the child spinning the *lariat*.

When all of the children have had a turn, put the *lariat* away and say: **God loves each of us so much that he protects us. Whenever you're scared, you can think about the circle of protection that God gives you. Let's thank God.**

Pray: **God, we thank you for protecting us. Help us remember that you take care of us when we're afraid.**

### Teacher Tip

If the *lariat's* plastic streamer is too long for children to twirl, trim the streamer to a length of 6 feet.

## ELIJAH 4:
**God protects us when we're afraid.**

### KEY VERSE

*"The Lord is my strength and shield. I trust him, and he helps me. I am very happy, and I praise him with my song"* (Psalm 28:7).

# GROWING TOGETHER

## I·N T·O·U·C·H

Today the first- and second-graders learned that God will protect them when they're scared. The children learned that all of us have fears we want to hide from or run away from. But the children also learned to give all their worries to God because God cares about them. Use these ideas to help your child overcome his or her fears.

## FEARS

Some kinds of fear are good for us because they keep us safe. For example, it's good for children to be somewhat afraid of the kind of danger posed by busy traffic. Other kinds of fear, such as speaking in public, can be conquered. Think of scary things together and decide whether the situations are dangerous or just difficult. Tell your child that it's important to avoid dangerous situations. Remind your child that God protects us as we grow and learn and that he helps us make wise choices in dangerous situations.

## SHADOWS

Go outside on a day when you can see your shadow. Take turns jumping on each other's shadows and trying to jump on your own. No matter how many times your shadows get stomped, they can't be stopped. Tell your child that even though very scary things threaten to stomp on us, under God's protection we're as safe as our shadows on a sunny day.

## ANGELS

Instead of a soft, ethereal angel, create this tough-as-nails angel to teach your child that angels are strong enough to protect us from any danger we face. Read Psalm 91:11. Then draw an angel on a piece of wood. Follow the example in the illustration. Gather old nails, screws, bolts, washers, and thumbtacks. Help your child hammer the nails or push in thumbtacks to form the outline of the angel. Glue on bolts, washers, nails, and screws to fill in the body. If you don't have these kinds of scraps, build

a strong angel with building blocks or rocks. Talk about the dangers angels protect us from and how strong angels must be.

## SAFE NIGHTS

Together, memorize Psalm 4:8. As you tuck your child into bed each night, talk about how God kept you safe that day. Then pray the verse together.

# I·N H·I·S H·A·N·D·S

## THE POINT
God is in control of the future.

It's important to say The Point just as it's written in each activity. Repeating The Point over and over will help children remember it and apply it to their lives.

## THE BIBLE BASIS:
2 Kings 2:1-14. Elijah goes to heaven.

Elijah's life on earth ends in this passage. But what a way to go! Elijah and his protégé, Elisha, knew that the day had come for Elijah to go to heaven. Elisha wanted to be present at Elijah's departure. He refused to be separated from Elijah on that day. And when other prophets brought up the subject of Elijah's departure, Elisha refused to talk about it. But soon Elisha had to face losing his friend and mentor. As they walked and talked, a chariot and horses of fire appeared and separated them. Elijah was taken into heaven by a whirlwind, and Elisha received a double portion of Elijah's spirit as an inheritance. Both were taken care of by God. Both had secure futures.

Children today start worrying as soon as they are old enough to walk. Why? Because parents show them how. "Where should he go to preschool?" "Should she start piano lessons when she's 4 or 5?" Children feel a great deal of stress when they think about the future. They face going to school, getting good grades, pleasing teachers and parents, making friends, fitting in, and growing up.

It's fun, but it's scary and overwhelming, too. It's comforting to know that God's in charge. This lesson will reassure children that God's mighty hand is holding theirs. Thanks to God, we can all face tomorrow!

Other Scriptures used in this lesson are Proverbs 3:5-6 and Hebrews 6:17-18.

## KEY VERSE
for Lessons 1–5

"The Lord is my strength and shield. I trust him, and he helps me. I am very happy, and I praise him with my song" (Psalm 28:7).

# GETTING THE POINT

Children will

- see that worrying about the future takes joy out of their lives;
- learn that when they depend on God, their paths will be straightened; and
- see that God took care of the past and will take care of the future.

cheetos

Before the lesson, collect the items from the Learning Lab for the activities you plan to use. Refer to the pictures in the margin to see what each item looks like.

# THIS LESSON AT A GLANCE

| SECTION | MINUTES | WHAT CHILDREN WILL DO | LEARNING LAB SUPPLIES | CLASSROOM SUPPLIES |
|---|---|---|---|---|
| WELCOME TIME | up to 5 | **Welcome!**—Receive a warm welcome from the teacher and make name tags. | | "Trust God" name tags (p. 25), markers, scissors, tape |
| ATTENTION GRABBER | up to 10 | **Bugs and Balls**—Predict how many bugs they can knock off a table with a ball and see that God's knowledge is limitless while theirs is limited. | Black insects, return ball | |
| BIBLE EXPLORATION & APPLICATION | up to 13 | **Elijah and Elisha**—Hear the story of Elijah's going to heaven and see that God took care of Elisha's future just as God will take care of their futures. | | Bible |
| | up to 10 | **Past and Future**—Talk about what God has done in the past and their worries for the future and be reassured by Hebrews 6:17-18 that God will take care of them. | | Bible |
| | up to 12 | **Straightened Paths**—Walk along a crooked path, read Proverbs 3:5-6, and discover that God will be with them and will straighten their paths when they rely on him. | Jump-rope | Bible |
| CLOSING | up to 10 | **Joy-Biters**—Talk about their worries and thank God for promising to take care of the future. | Castanets | |

Remember to make photocopies of the "Growing Together" handout (p. 66) to send home with your children. "Growing Together" is a valuable tool for helping first- and second-graders talk with their parents about what they're learning in class.

# T·H·E L·E·S·S·O·N

## **W**ELCOME TIME

### WELCOME!

**(up to 5 minutes)**

- Greet each child individually with an enthusiastic smile.
- Thank each child for coming to class today.
- As children arrive, ask them about last week's "Growing Together" discussion. Use questions such as "What did you do to learn about God's care?" and "What did you discover about being afraid?"
- Say: **Today we're going to learn that** ⭐ **God is in control of the future.**
- Help children put on their name tags. If some children weren't in class last week, or if some of the name tags were damaged, photocopy the "Trust God" name tags (p. 25) and have children follow the instructions to create new name tags.
- Tell the children that the attention-getting signal you'll use during this lesson is clapping your hands three times. Ask children to respond by clapping their hands three times as they stop talking and focus their attention on you. Rehearse the signal with the children, telling them to respond quickly so you have plenty of time for all the fun activities planned for this lesson.

**THE POINT** ⭐

## **A**TTENTION GRABBER

### BUGS AND BALLS

**(up to 10 minutes)**

**LEARNING LAB**

Scatter the *black insects* on a table top. Show the children the *return ball.* Say: **This ball bounces all over the place. You never know where it will bounce next, so this game will be fun. Each of us will get 10 tries to bounce as many bugs as possible off the table with the *return ball.* You can fling the ball sideways to hit the bugs, or you can bounce the ball from straight above the table. You can fling the ball from far away or from up close. Anything goes, as long as you don't touch the bugs with your hands.**

As children take turns, have them guess how many bugs they'll bounce off the table. Before the children bounce the ball, have them slide the plastic ring over one of their fingers so that the ball will return to them after it's bounced. Praise each child's attempts to hit the bugs. After each child's turn, replace any bugs that are knocked off the table.

When everyone has had a turn, return the *black insects* and the *return ball* to the Learning Lab. Ask:

● **Was it easy or hard to guess what the ball was going to do? Why?** (It was tough because the ball never went where I thought it would; it was hard because I was only right once.)

● **It was tough to predict what would happen in this game. Have you ever tried to predict what would happen in your life? What happened?** (I thought it would snow during the night, but it didn't; once I thought I knew what my parents were getting me for Christmas, and I was right.)

● **Why can't we always be right when we predict the future?** (Because we're not God; because we can't see the future; because nobody knows the future.)

Say: **We never knew for sure how many bugs we could hit. We could guess, and sometimes we were right, but we never knew for sure. We just had to wait and see what would happen, because we can't see into the future. Sometimes we'd like to know what is going to happen, because it's easy to worry about the future. Today we're going to find out what happened to someone who was worried about the future. He found out, just as we'll find out, that there's nothing to worry about because ★ God is in control of the future.**

 **THE POINT**

# BIBLE EXPLORATION & APPLICATION

## ELIJAH AND ELISHA 📖

### (up to 13 minutes)

Show children the story in 2 Kings 2:1-14.

Say: **We've been talking a lot about a man named Elijah. Today the story gets complicated because we're going to talk about Elijah again, but we're also going to talk about Elisha, who was another prophet. Those names sound so much alike that you'll need to listen carefully to know who does what. To make it easier, every time I say "Elijah," point to heaven because that's where Elijah goes in the story today. Whenever I say "Elisha," wring your hands to show that Elisha is worried.**

**Let's practice that. Elijah.** Have the children point to heaven. **Elisha.** Have the children wring their hands.

Good. Let's tell the story.

It was almost time for God to take Elijah (have the children point to heaven) **up to heaven in a whirlwind.** (Have the children swirl their arms in front of them like a whirlwind.)

Elijah (have the children point to heaven) **said to his friend Elisha** (have children wring their hands), **"I need to go to Bethel. Please stay here while I'm gone."**

But Elisha (have children wring their hands) **said, "As surely as you're alive, I will not leave you."**

So together, the two men traveled to Bethel.

There were other prophets there who took Elisha (wring hands) **aside and said, "Don't you know that today is the day that Elijah** (point to heaven) **will go to heaven?"**

Elisha (wring hands) **said, "Yes, I know, but please don't talk to me about it."**

Then Elijah (point to heaven) **said, "Now God is sending me to Jericho. You stay here."**

But Elisha (wring hands) **said again, "As surely as you're alive, I will not leave you."**

So together, they traveled to Jericho. More prophets came out and said to Elisha (wring hands), **"Don't you know that God will take Elijah** (point to heaven) **to heaven today?"**

And again, Elisha (wring hands) **said, "Yes, I know about it. But please, please don't talk about it."**

Next, Elijah (point to heaven) **said, "God has sent me to the Jordan River. You stay here."**

But again, Elisha (wring hands) **said, "As surely as God lives, I won't leave you."**

So they went together to the Jordan River. Fifty men from the groups of prophets stood far off and watched. Elijah (point to heaven) **took off his coat, rolled it up, and hit the water with it. The water divided to the right and to the left, and the two men crossed the river on dry ground.**

When they had crossed over, Elijah (point to heaven) **asked Elisha** (wring hands), **"Before I go, what can I do for you?"**

Elisha (wring hands) **said, "I'd like to be like you. I want to carry on your ministry as a prophet after you've gone."**

Elijah (point to heaven) **said, "You've asked for a difficult thing. But if you see me as I'm taken from you, you will get what you've asked for."**

As the two men were walking and talking, a chariot and horses made of fire appeared and separated them. Elijah (point to heaven) **was taken up to heaven in a whirlwind.** (Make a whirlwind motion in front of you.)

Elisha (wring hands) **saw Elijah** (point to heaven) **rise in the air.** Elisha (wring hands) **ripped his clothes to show how sad he was that his friend was going away.**

He picked up Elijah's (point to heaven) **coat, which had fallen. Then he stood on the banks of the river.**

**BIBLE INSIGHT**

According to Old Testament custom, the first-born son received a double share of the father's inheritance (Deuteronomy 21:17). In asking for a double share of Elijah's spirit, Elisha was asking to be Elijah's heir, the one who would continue Elijah's work as leader of the prophets.

He hit the water with the coat, just as he had seen Elijah (point to heaven) **do. The river divided to the left and to the right, just as it had done for Elijah.** (Point to heaven.)

And he knew that he had inherited Elijah's (point to heaven) **ministry, just as he had been promised. Ask:**

● **Why do you think Elisha was worried about the future?** (He was worried because he knew his friend was going away; he was worried because he didn't know what would happen to him when Elijah went away.)

Say: **Elisha didn't want to talk about Elijah leaving. But it's good to talk things over when we're worried. Ask:**

● **Who do you talk to about your worries?** (My mom; my grandpa; my teacher; my best friend; God.)

● **What do they do that comforts you?** (They hug me; they tell me that everything will be OK; they listen to me.)

● **What did Elijah do to comfort Elisha?** (He let Elisha inherit his ministry.)

 **THE POINT**

Say: **Elisha knew that Elijah was going to heaven. What Elisha didn't know was what would happen to him after Elijah left. Elisha didn't want to be without his friend. But** ★ **God is in control of the future. God took care of Elisha by giving him what he needed to take over Elijah's ministry. Elijah's spirit helped make Elisha a strong and powerful prophet. God will take care of us in the future, too. Let's find out more.**

## PAST AND FUTURE 📖

### (up to 10 minutes)

### Teacher Tip

If your class has an uneven number of children, participate in this activity yourself. If your class has fewer than six members, have children form pairs to do this activity. If you have fewer than four students, have the children work as a group.

Have the class form two circles, an inner circle and an outer circle. Have the children stand so that each person in the inner circle is facing a person in the outer circle.

Say: **If you're on the inside circle, tell the person you're standing across from one good thing that you know God has done in the past. It can be something from the Bible or from your life. For example, you might say, "God created the world" or "God helped my mom get better when she was sick."**

Give children a minute to share information with their partners. Then have the inside partner say, "God took care of the past," as partners exchange high fives with their right hands.

Say: **If you're on the outside circle, tell your partner on the inside something good that you hope God will do in the future. You might say, "I hope God will help me become a doctor when I grow up" or "I hope God will help my neighbor not get so angry at me."**

 **THE POINT**

Have the outside partner say, "And ★ God is in control of the future," as partners exchange high fives with their left hands.

Have children in the outside circle rotate to the right until they're each in front of the next person on the inside circle. This time, have the children in the outside circle tell about something that God has done in the past and have the children on the inside circle tell about the future. Have them exchange high fives in the same manner as before.

Then have the children on the inside circle move to the left one place. Continue rotating the circle and sharing as time permits. Then have the children sit down. Ask:

● **What are some of the exciting things God has done in the past?** (God created the world; God sent Jesus; God parted the Red Sea.)

● **How do we know that God will do good things in the future, too?** (Because God promises to take care of us; because God is God; because God is good.)

Say: **Listen to these verses from the Bible.** Read Hebrews 6:17-18. Ask:

● **What do these verses say that God will never do?** (God will never lie; God will never break his promises.)

● **What does God promise to do for us?** (God promises to take care of us; God promises to feed us; God promises to be with us when we're scared.)

Say: **God doesn't promise to do everything just as we want them done. But God does promise to take care of us and to do what's best for us. And now we know that God always keeps his promises. That's great news. We can be excited about what will happen to us because ✦ God is in control of the future.**

## KEY VERSE Connection

"The Lord is my strength and shield. I trust him, and he helps me. I am very happy, and I praise him with my song" (Psalm 28:7).

Elijah trusted God, and God protected Elijah, fed him, directed him, and comforted him throughout his life. When he was older, Elijah was assigned by God to teach at the schools of the prophets. He left his future in God's hands and traveled anywhere God led him, finally to the Jordan River, where he was "taken up" in faith and trust.

# STRAIGHTENED PATHS 📖

## (up to 12 minutes)

Put the *jump-rope* on the floor in a very crooked line. Say: **This is a crooked path. Let's all try walking along it with our eyes closed. Go slowly and balance yourself carefully.**

Have children take turns closing their eyes and walking along the crooked path.

When everyone has had a turn, have children sit down where they can't reach the *jump-rope*. Say: **Let's pretend that the crooked path is actually the road of our lives.** Ask:

● **What was it like to walk on the crooked path?** (It was hard to know where to go; I kept falling off.)

● **What are some things that would make the road of our lives crooked and difficult to walk along?** (Evil people; bad things like storms.)

Say: **We all know that ✦ God is in control of the future. Listen to this passage from the Bible and be ready to tell me what happens to the crooked path when we trust God.** Read Proverbs 3:5-6 from the New International Version. Ask:

**LEARNING LAB**

**THE POINT**

● **What happens to the path when we trust God?** (It becomes straight.)

Straighten the *jump-rope* and have the children walk along it with their eyes closed again. Ask:

● **Was it easier to walk on the path this time? Why?** (It was easier because I knew where it would go; it was easier, but I still fell off.)

Say: **God doesn't promise to take all our troubles away. But when we trust God to take care of the future, he helps us face whatever comes along. And when we trust God, we can be sure that he's with us.**

Return the *jump-rope* to the Learning Lab.

**W**e believe Christian education extends beyond the classroom into the home. Photocopy the "Growing Together" handout (p. 66) for this week and send it home with your children. Encourage children and parents to use the handout to plan meaningful activities on this week's topic. Follow up the "Growing Together" activities next week by asking children what their families did.

# C LOSING

## JOY-BITERS

**(up to 10 minutes)**

Ask:

● **What did you learn today?** (I learned that God's in control of the future; I learned that God will take care of me just as he took care of people in the Bible.)

Show the *castanets* to the children. Hold them sideways and click them together so they look like a mouth biting. Say: **Sometimes we worry about things. We worry about things that will happen for sure and we worry about things that might happen. We worry about big things and little things. Everyone worries about the future. And when we worry, it's hard to be happy and joyful. Let's call these *castanets* joy-biters. They show that when we worry, we lose some of our joy.**

**Let's take turns clicking the joy-biters as we talk about the things that worry us. Since ★ God is in control of the future, though, we can stop worrying. So after you say what you worry about and click the joy-biters, hold them shut with your other hand so they can't bite any**

more of your joy. Then say, "I don't need to worry because ✦ God is in control of the future."

When everyone has had a chance to share, say: **God cares enough about us that he has made plans for our future. We can be full of joy because of God's plans.** Have the children clap and cheer for the future that God has planned for them.

Pray: **God, sometimes we get scared and worried about what might happen to us in the future. But you already know what's going to happen, and you promise to take care of us. Help us to remember that you're in control and we can trust you. We're excited and ready for the future because we know you're in charge. Thank you for loving us enough to take care of us. We can be excited about the future. Thanks, God. Amen.**

## ELIJAH 5:

God is in control of the future.

### KEY VERSE

*"The Lord is my strength and shield. I trust him, and he helps me. I am very happy, and I praise him with my song"* (Psalm 28:7).

# GROWING TOGETHER

Permission to photocopy this handout from Group's Hands-On Bible Curriculum™ for Grades 1 and 2 granted for local church use. Copyright © Group Publishing, Inc., P.O. Box 481, Loveland, CO 80539.

## I·N T·O·U·C·H

Today your child learned that there's no need to worry about what might happen, because God is in control of the future. The children learned that God doesn't change and he'll take care of us just as he took care of his people in the Bible. Use these activities to excite your child about the future.

## THE TOP 10

Make a list of your top-10 worries about the future. Then pray about them. Take turns reading from the list, then say together, "But we know you're in charge of the future. Thank you, God." For example, your child might pray, "God, I'm worried about having a new teacher next fall." Then pray together, "But we know you're in control of the future. Thank you, God."

## GOD'S GUIDANCE

Create a spider-web maze through your home with a ball of string or yarn. You might tie the string to the banister, then stretch it across the living room, around the coffee table, and so on around the house until it ends up at the kitchen table. Make the maze complicated so that it will take your child at least five minutes to follow the maze to its end. Hide a treat at the end of the maze. Have your child follow the maze. Then read Isaiah 42:16 and talk about how God guides us through life. What rewards do we get in the future when we follow God? What rewards do we enjoy along the way?

## CHARIOTS OF FIRE

A chariot of fire appeared when Elijah was taken to heaven in a whirlwind. Make these fast chariots. For each chariot, you'll need a small paper cup and a marble. Use scissors to cut the cups to look like the chariot in the illustration below. Cut people out of construction paper and tape them inside the back of the chariots.

Place the chariots over marbles at one end of a cookie sheet.

Guess which one will win. Tilt the cookie sheet gently and watch the chariots fly. Talk about how God knows what will happen in the future but our knowledge is limited.

## MUSICAL MOMENT

Sing this song to the tune of "Jesus Loves Me":

God has made a plan for you.
He knows what you will go through.
Follow him through every day.
God will guide you all the way.
God knows the future.
God knows the future.
God knows the future,
And he will care for you.

# E·Z·R·A A·N·D N·E·H·E·M·I·A·H

The people of Judah were held as captives of war in Babylon for 70 years. Then the Persians conquered Babylon, and the new king let the captives return to their homeland. God chose Ezra and Nehemiah to lead the people who chose to return and re-establish Israel. Ezra led the people in rebuilding the temple. He also reminded the Jews of their spiritual heritage and brought them into a new awareness of what God had done for them.

The Jews learned a lot when they returned to Jerusalem. There were ruins to rebuild and a city to fortify. As the people worked together, they learned to put God first and to treat others with fairness. Most important, they made a solemn commitment to live for God. These lessons are important to the children in your class, too. Use these stories from the lives of Ezra and Nehemiah to help your students learn to work together and to work for God.

## FOUR LESSONS ON EZRA AND NEHEMIAH

| LESSON | PAGE | THE POINT | THE BIBLE BASIS |
|---|---|---|---|
| 6—GOD FIRST | 73 | God wants us to put him first. | Ezra 3:1–6:16 |
| 7—WORK TOGETHER | 85 | God wants us to work together for him. | Nehemiah 3:1–4:23; 6:1-15 |
| 8—KIND TO ALL | 95 | God wants us to help people who are being treated unfairly. | Nehemiah 5:1-13 |
| 9—LIVE FOR GOD | 105 | We can decide to live for God. | Nehemiah 8:1–10:39 |

#  HE SIGNAL

During the lessons on Ezra and Nehemiah your attention-getting signal will be clapping your hands three times. Have children respond by clapping their hands three times as they stop talking and focus their attention on you. Tell children about this signal before the lesson begins. Explain that it's important to respond to this signal quickly so the class can do as many fun activities as possible.

#  HE FIDGET BUSTER

Use this activity when you need to provide an action break for wigglers and squirmers. Say: **When I say, "Build the wall," run to the center of the room and pile your fists on top of each other's fists until you make a towering wall of fists. You must hurry to build the wall before I count to 10.**

Have the children stand in a large circle. Call out: **Build the wall!** Count to 10, then tell the children to return to their places in the circle.

Play the game several times but vary the instructions each time. For example, you might call out "two-person wall" and have each person build a fist wall with a partner. You can call out "three-person wall" or "four-person wall," too. End as you began by having everyone build one wall of fists together. Then return to your lesson.

#  HE TIME STUFFER

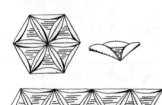

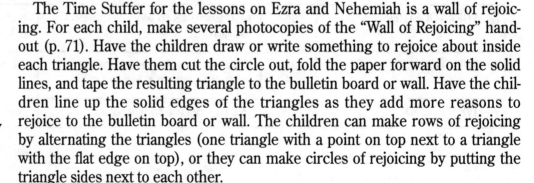

The Time Stuffer for the lessons on Ezra and Nehemiah is a wall of rejoicing. For each child, make several photocopies of the "Wall of Rejoicing" handout (p. 71). Have the children draw or write something to rejoice about inside each triangle. Have them cut the circle out, fold the paper forward on the solid lines, and tape the resulting triangle to the bulletin board or wall. Have the children line up the solid edges of the triangles as they add more reasons to rejoice to the bulletin board or wall. The children can make rows of rejoicing by alternating the triangles (one triangle with a point on top next to a triangle with the flat edge on top), or they can make circles of rejoicing by putting the triangle sides next to each other.

# REMEMBERING GOD'S WORD

Key verse: "God chose you to be his people, so I urge you now to live the life to which God called you" (Ephesians 4:1b).

This module's verse will help children learn to live in a way that pleases God. Use these activities any time during the lessons on Ezra and Nehemiah.

## CHOSEN PEOPLE

Before class, set up a circle of chairs. Be sure to have a chair for each child. Write an X on a 3×5 card for each child. Fold each card in half so the X isn't visible. Tape a card to the underside of each chair.

Say: **Pick a chair to sit in. Choose your chair carefully because if there is an X on the card taped to the bottom of your chair, then you will win a prize.**

When everyone has chosen a chair, tell children to look at the cards to see if they are marked with an X.

Give each child a cookie for a prize. Ask:

● **What did you think when you realized that everyone's card has an X on it?** (I was surprised because I thought there was only one prize; I knew that everyone would win.)

Say: **Listen to what the Bible says.** Read Ephesians 4:1b.

Say: **Each of you was chosen to receive a prize in this game, and God has chosen Christians to receive something from him.** Ask:

● **What does it mean that God chose us to be his people?** (It means that God loves us; it means that we're God's children; it means that God picked us.)

● **How do you feel, knowing that God chose us?** (I feel good; I feel special; I feel important.)

● **How is that feeling like the feeling you get when you win a prize?** (When I get a prize, I'm happy, too; both make me feel good.)

● **The verse also says that we should live the life that we've been called to. How can you live that kind of life?** (I can do good things; I can obey God; I can love other people.)

Say: **God chose us to be his. That means we get to be God's children and we can live with him forever in heaven if we have faith in Jesus. It also means that we will live to please God and to show his love to other people. Let's say the verse together to help us remember what we've learned.**

Say Ephesians 4:1b together.

## PICKED BY GOD

Write every child's name on a piece of paper and put the papers in the Learning Lab box.

Stand at the front of the room. Have the children spread out around the room and face the back of the room.

Say: **Listen to my instructions and do what I say when I pull your name out of the box and call out to you.**

Pull a name out of the box and say: (Child's name), **I choose you to turn around and face me. I choose you to point to heaven.** Prompt this child to follow your instructions and repeat them throughout the game.

Pull each child's name out of the box; tell the child to turn and face you; then give each child a different, quiet action to do, such as rubbing his or her tummy or patting the ground. When every child is doing an action, stop the game.

Gather the children and have them sit down. Ask:

● **How did you feel when you were waiting to be called?** (I felt left out; I was nervous because I didn't know what my action would be; I felt funny facing away from you.)

● **How did you feel when I called your name?** (Happy to have something to do; I was glad I wasn't left out.)

● **What did you think about the action you had to do? Did you like it? Did you get tired of it?** (I thought my action was silly, but it was fun; I got kind of tired because I was the first person called and I had to do my action the longest.)

Read Ephesians 4:1b.

● **What do you think it means that God chose us?** (It means that God wants us to be Christians; it means that God loves us.)

● **How can you live the life you were called to live?** (I can keep obeying God; I can pay attention to God like I paid attention to you in the game.)

● **What kinds of things can you do to show that you're living the life you were called to?** (I can obey; I can love others; I can be kind; I can be fair.)

Say: **Let's say the verse together to remind us that God picked us.** Say Ephesians 4:1b together.

# WALL OF REJOICING

Make several photocopies of this page for each child. Put the photocopies in an area with tape, markers, and scissors. Have the children write or draw a reason for rejoicing in each triangle then cut out each circle and fold on the lines of the triangle. Attach the triangles to a bulletin board or wall.

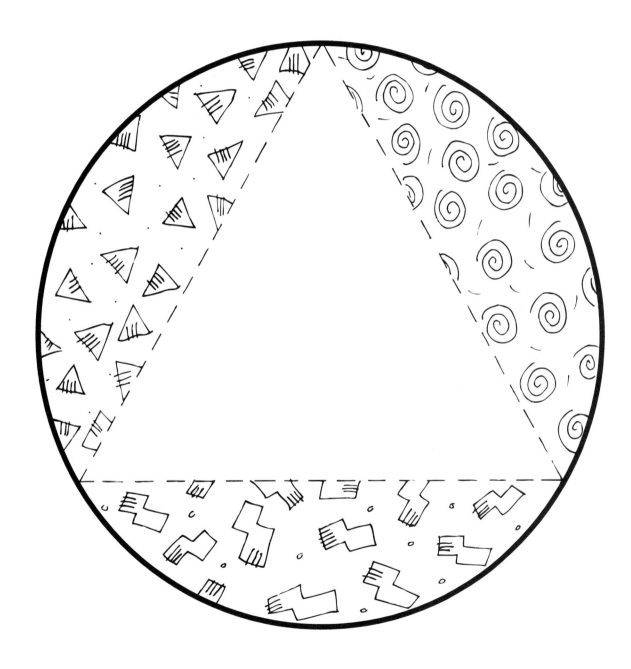

# W·O·R·K
# T·O·G·E·T·H·E·R July 13

## THE POINT
God wants us to work together for him.

It's important to say The Point just as it's written in each activity. Repeating The Point over and over will help children remember it and apply it to their lives.

## THE BIBLE BASIS: 📖
Nehemiah 3:1–4:23; 6:1-15. Nehemiah rebuilds the wall.

When Nehemiah heard that his homeland was in ruins, he was overcome with a sadness that led him to prayer and planning. He was a highly respected servant in the king's court, and he mustered the courage to ask King Artaxerxes for permission to return to Jerusalem and rebuild the wall around the city. Artaxerxes granted permission, and Nehemiah soon left for Jerusalem. When he arrived, he organized work crews and gathered supplies for the job. His leadership turned a group of individuals into a hard-working community that accomplished an amazing task. Nehemiah's work crews built a defensible wall around the entire city of Jerusalem in only 52 days.

Nehemiah's story provides great lessons for first- and second-graders. They are just beginning to feel part of a group. They thrive on group games, but they're still learning how to interact successfully in work groups. Nehemiah's story can help first- and second-graders see that people who work together and do their parts with enthusiasm can accomplish great feats. This lesson will help children understand that working together can be fun, too.

Other Scriptures used in this lesson are Ecclesiastes 4:9-12; Galatians 6:9; and Ephesians 4:12-13.

## KEY VERSE
### for Lessons 6–9

"God chose you to be his people, so I urge you now to live the life to which God called you" (Ephesians 4:1b).

# GETTING THE POINT

Children will

● work together to build a wall around a temple,

● discover that they can accomplish more when they work together, and

● see that they can combine their gifts with other people's gifts to bring God's message to others.

Before the lesson, collect the items from the Learning Lab for the activities you plan to use. Refer to the pictures in the margin to see what each item looks like.

## THIS LESSON AT A GLANCE

| SECTION | MINUTES | WHAT CHILDREN WILL DO | LEARNING LAB SUPPLIES | CLASSROOM SUPPLIES |
|---------|---------|----------------------|----------------------|-------------------|
| WELCOME TIME | up to 5 | **Welcome!**—Receive a warm welcome from the teacher and make name tags. | | "Temple of God" name tags (p. 83), markers, scissors, tape |
| ATTENTION GRABBER | up to 10 | **Defend the Spider**—Play a game in which they work together to defend or steal a spider, then discuss why working together makes good sense. | Spider web, spider | Paper |
| BIBLE EXPLORATION & APPLICATION | up to 13 | **Building the Wall**—Build a wall to defend a temple and learn how Nehemiah and the Jews worked together to build a wall around Jerusalem. | | Bible, temple from Lesson 6, (newspaper,) tape |
| | up to 10 | **Bug Messages**—Work together to solve a problem, read Galatians 6:9, and discover the rewards of working together. | Black insect | Bible, paper, paper clips, treats, pencil, tape *gold fish* |
| | up to 12 | **Three Strands**—Read Ecclesiastes 4:9-12 and learn from braiding three strands together that they're stronger when they work with others. | Burlap | Bible, tape |
| CLOSING | up to 10 | **Ability Combinations**—Discuss how they could put their gifts together in new and exciting ways to work together for the kingdom of God. | Paint set, paint-brushes | Bible |

Remember to make photocopies of the "Growing Together" handout (p. 94) to send home with your children. "Growing Together" is a valuable tool for helping first- and second-graders talk with their parents about what they're learning in class.

# T·H·E  L·E·S·S·O·N

## **W**ELCOME TIME

### WELCOME!
**(up to 5 minutes)**

● Greet each child individually with an enthusiastic smile.
● Thank each child for coming to class today.
● As children arrive, ask them about last week's "Growing Together" discussion. Use questions such as "How did you put God first last week?" and "How did you worship God with your family?"
● Say: **Today we're going to learn that**  **God wants us to work together for him.**
● Help children put on their name tags. If some children weren't in class last week, or if some of the name tags were damaged, photocopy the "Temple of God" name tags (p. 83) and have children follow the instructions to create new name tags.
● Tell the children that the attention-getting signal you'll use during this lesson is clapping your hands three times. Ask children to respond by clapping their hands three times as they stop talking and focus their attention on you. Rehearse the signal with the children, telling them to respond quickly so you have plenty of time for all the fun activities planned for this lesson.

**THE POINT**

## **A**TTENTION GRABBER

### DEFEND THE SPIDER
**(up to 10 minutes)**

Wad up the *spider web,* put the *spider* on top of it, and place it in the center of the room. Place sheets of paper in a circle around the web. Space the papers so that children standing on them won't be able to touch each other.

Form two teams: the protectors and the raiders. Have each protector stand on one sheet of paper. Say: **Protectors, your job is to protect the *spider* from the raiders. You can use your arms, but your feet can't move from the papers. The raiders will try to steal the *spider* and bring it to me. Ready? Go!**

**LEARNING LAB**

It should be easy for the raiders to steal the *spider* from the middle of the circle. When they do, congratulate them and ask them:

● **What made it easy to steal the *spider*?** (We could just walk in and grab it; the protectors couldn't keep us out of the circle.)

Ask the protectors:

● **What made it hard to defend the *spider*?** (There was no way for us to keep the raiders out of the circle; we were too far apart.)

● **What could we do to make it easier to keep the raiders out of the circle?** (We could stand closer together; we could change the rules so we can move around the circle; we could join our arms together so the raiders would have a tougher time getting through.)

Together choose one of the strategies the protectors suggest. Then have them defend the *spider* from the raiders. After 30 seconds or so, have the teams switch places. Have the new protectors devise a new way to protect the *spider.* Have them work together to try their idea. Then put the *spider,* the web, and the sheets of paper away. Ask:

● **Why was it easier to defend the *spider* this time?** (Because we could work together; because we stood closer together.)

Say: **Today we're going to talk about a group of people who had a problem similar to ours. They had a city to protect: Jerusalem. But the wall around the city had been torn down. It was in ruins, and there were huge gaps in it that would let enemies in. These people learned that ✦ God wants us to work together for him. Let's find out how the people worked together to defend their city.**

 **THE POINT**

## BIBLE EXPLORATION & APPLICATION

### BUILDING THE WALL 📖

**(up to 13 minutes)**

You'll need newspaper, tape, and the temple the children built in Lesson 6.

Have the children form a circle and sit about a foot apart from each other. Put the temple in the middle of the circle. Open your Bible to Nehemiah 3. Say: **A man named Nehemiah went to Jerusalem to help the Jews rebuild the wall around the city and the finished temple.**

**He rode around the city and found out exactly what needed to be done. Then he gathered workers and gave everyone a section of the wall to rebuild. Some parts of the old wall were still in good condition, but in places the wall had to be completely rebuilt. Let's build our own wall.**

Give each child some newspaper. Have each child wad up sheets of paper and tape them together to form a wall section that's about 1 foot high, 1 foot deep, and 2 feet long. The children will attach their sections together later in the activity.

Even if the children aren't finished after two or three minutes of work, clap three times and wait for the children to stop working, clap their hands three times, and focus their attention on you. Say: **While the people were busily working on the wall, they found out that it worked better if different people had different jobs. Some people started to work on the wooden parts of the gates and walls. Others repaired the stone parts of the walls. Let's see how it works to divide up the jobs.**

Appoint two or three children to tear off tape segments. Appoint several others to crumple newspaper. Have the rest of the children tape the wads together to continue building the sections of the wall that have already been started. Don't let them join the sections together yet. If one group gets ahead or behind the rest, move kids from job to job to even out the tasks.

After two or three minutes, stop the work again by clapping your hands three times. Wait for children to respond, then ask:

● **Was it easier or harder to do the work after we split up the jobs?** (It was easier because I didn't always have to go find the tape; it was harder because I had to wait for newspaper wads and tape.)

Say: **After the people were working on the wall, Nehemiah found out that enemies didn't want the wall to be finished. They were ready to do anything to stop the work. So some of the people had to work as guards. They carried weapons and watched in case the enemies tried to start a fight. The enemies made fun of the workers and said that the wall would never hold. But Nehemiah and the other workers just kept on working. They worked from the time the sun rose in the morning until the stars came out at night.**

Have the children resume their work on the wall, with each child doing the job he or she was assigned earlier. When the sections are 1 foot high, 1 foot deep, and 2 feet long, have the children join the sections together to form a wall around the temple.

Say: **After only 52 days of hard work, the people finished the wall. The people had worked long hours, but they had worked together, and they had accomplished a great thing. Jerusalem and the new temple were now safe from enemy attacks. When all of the enemies and all of the other countries saw what the Jews had done, they were ashamed. The enemies saw that God had been with the Jews as they rebuilt the wall.** Ask:

● **How did working together help the Jews build the wall?** (It helped them get the job done more quickly; everyone did a little bit to help finish it.)

● **How did working together help us build our wall?** (It helped to have people do different things so we didn't have to do it all ourselves; together we were able to build a big wall instead of the small wall we would have built by ourselves.)

● **When do you work with others?** (In church; in school; at home.)

● **What kinds of things do you do with others?** (Our choir has lots of people in it; we cleaned up the playground, and that took a lot of people.)

# BIBLE INSIGHT

Nehemiah required each worker to build up the city wall behind or opposite that person's own house. Each person could see the importance of the wall, and people were motivated to quickly and properly finish their sections. Nehemiah made all the workers feel as if the wall were their own. They worked together for God, the city, and personal satisfaction.

● **How can you work together with others more?** (I can offer to help others; I can work to get along with other people better.)

Say: **Big projects are easier to accomplish when many people work together. If you had built this wall around the temple by yourself, it would have taken you much longer than it took with our whole class working on it. God wants us to accomplish many things in the world. He wanted the Jews to work together to build a wall around Jerusalem. ✦ God wants us to work together for him, too.**

# BUG MESSAGES 📖

## (up to 10 minutes)

**KEY VERSE**
Connection

"God chose you to be his people, so I urge you now to live the life to which God called you" (Ephesians 4:1b).

God gives us our talents and abilities so that we are equipped to do the tasks he gives us. He has a plan for each of us to use these talents as we work together for his glory.

Before class, <u>hide a treat somewhere in the room</u>.

Designate a starting line on one side of the room and a finish line on the opposite side of the room. Give each child a sheet of paper and two paper clips. Show the children how to roll the paper lengthwise and clip it with the paper clips so that it doesn't come unrolled. Roll the paper so that the diameter is about as big as a half dollar.

While children are rolling up their papers, print the location of the treat on a small slip of paper, fold the paper as many times as you can, and tape it securely to one of the *black insects*.

Say: **This bug has a message to deliver to a person at the finish line. To deliver the message, the bug must move from the starting line to the finish line through the paper rolls that you've just made. Let's pretend that the floor is covered with water. We're OK because we're tall. But if the bug falls out of the paper rolls, it will drown before the message is delivered.**

**Let's put the ends of the paper rolls together to form a pipeline. Will it reach all the way to the finish line?**

Have the children line up at the starting line and put their papers together to form a pipeline. Don't tape the papers together; just have children hold the rolls in place. The pipeline probably won't reach the finish line—that's OK.

Put the bug in the pipeline and have the children shake it down to the last person in line. Then have the children think of ways to safely deliver the bug the rest of the way. Remind the children that the bug can't leave the pipeline. If several children offer suggestions, have all the children vote for the one they think will work best.

If the kids need help thinking of an idea, mention that the child at the starting line could move to the other end of the line to extend the pipeline. This process could be repeated until the pipeline and the bug reach the finish line.

When the bug reaches the finish line, have the person who delivered it there unfold the message and read it. Hand out the treats. Put away the bug and the paper rolls. While children are eating, ask:

● **What was it like to work together to get the bug across the room?**

Was it fun or frustrating? Explain. (I thought it was fun because everyone had good ideas; I thought it was hard because I didn't know what to do.)

● **Is it easy or hard to work together in real life?** (Sometimes it's easy because you like the person you're working with; it's easy if you agree, but it's hard if you fight; sometimes it's hard because you just want to do it by yourself.)

Say: **Listen to the Bible. Be ready to tell me what will happen if we don't give up.** Read Galatians 6:9. Ask:

● **What will happen if we don't give up?** (We'll get a harvest; we'll get eternal life.)

● **What did we gain or harvest by working together to get the bug to the finish line?** (We got treats; we felt good because we did a good job.)

● **What would have happened if some people had gotten tired and had refused to extend the pipeline?** (It would have been harder to get the bug to the end; it would have taken longer to get the treats.)

Say: **God has a special job for each of us to do.** ✦ **God wants us to work together for him. When we do, we'll accomplish more for him.** Ask:

THE POINT ★

● **What kinds of things might God want us to do together?** (Tell other people about him; treat others with kindness; build things; sing songs; learn about God.)

Say: **You've got great ideas on how to work together.** ✦ **God wants us to work together for him. When we do, we'll accomplish important things for God.**

THE POINT ★

# THREE STRANDS 📖

## (up to 12 minutes)

Before class, unravel enough of the *burlap* so that there are three strands for each child.

During class, say: **There's something else that you should know about working together. Listen while I read from the Bible.** Read Ecclesiastes 4:9-12.

Hold up a single strand of *burlap*. Say: **Suppose this is you by yourself. You can do a lot of great things by yourself.** Ask:

● **What can you do by yourself for God?** (I can pray; I can sing; I can tell others about God.)

Hold up two strands and say: **Now think of how much more you can do, how much more fun you can have, if you have a friend to work with.** Ask:

● **What can you do with a friend for God?** (We can sing and pray together; we can tell even more people about God; we can do more kind things for others.)

Hold up three strands and say: **Now imagine that there's a third person and that the third person is God. Think of all the things that three can do.** Ask:

● **What can you do with three or more?** (If God is helping, maybe we can do miracles; we can be even kinder; we can do many more good things for others.)

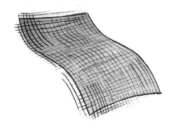
**LEARNING LAB**

Say: **This verse means that when we work together we can accomplish more things and we'll be stronger, too.**

Give a child a single strand of *burlap* and have him or her try to break it. It might break but only after a lot of effort. Then twist two strands together and have the child try to break that.

Give each child three strands of *burlap*. Have the children hold the pieces of *burlap* together and tape one end of the strands to a table so that the strands are lying on top of the table and the other ends are loose. Then have the children separate the three strands, placing one strand straight out to the right, the middle strand straight down, and the third strand straight out to the left.

Tell the children how to braid the strands. Say: **Pick up the right strand and lay it over the middle strand. Then pick up the left strand and put it over the strand that's in the middle. Keep putting the outside strands into the middle.** Help each child as necessary until everyone has about a 1-inch section of braid. Tape or knot the ends of the braids. Then ask:

● **How is this braid like us when we work together with God and others?** (We're stronger because we're together.)

Say: **Take these braids home as reminders to work with others to serve God. The more people work together, the more they will accomplish. They can help each other, and they'll have fun, too.** ✦ **God wants us to work together for him. Let's see how each of us can work with others to serve God.**

**THE POINT**

# CLOSING

## ABILITY COMBINATIONS 📖

### (up to 10 minutes)

Ask:
● **What did you learn today?** (I learned that working together is fun; I learned that God helps us when we work together; I learned that we can do good things for God when we work together.)

Put a few drops of water in each color of the *paint set* and let the paint soften. Swirl the paints with the *paintbrushes* so that a lot of the pigment is dissolved in the water.

Have the children form a circle. Using different colors for different children, brush a circle of paint on each child's hand. Have the children blow on their hands so that the paint dries. (The paint will wash off easily with soap and water.) It's OK if some children have the same color as others.

Say: **Listen while I read about what we can do when we work together.** Read Ephesians 4:12-13.

Say: **Think of a talent you have that you could use to serve God. For example, maybe you're good at putting on puppet shows, or maybe you sing well, or maybe you can draw well.** Have each child mention his or her ability. Be ready to mention ideas if the children have trouble thinking of their talents and abilities.

Say: ⭐ **God wants us to work together for him. Let's see what happens when we combine our gifts to work together for him. I'll call out colors. If I call the color on your hand, run to the middle of the circle and link arms with whoever else is there. Then we'll see what happens when we put your gifts together.**

Call out two colors—red and blue, for example. Have the children with red and blue spots on their hands rush to the center of the circle, link arms, and mention their gifts. Then have the class think of at least one way to combine their talents to work together for God. Encourage the children to think of fun, unusual, and imaginative ideas. For example, Sue and Brian might come forward. Sue rides horses, and Brian paints pictures. They could decide to have an art show on horseback in a parade that tells others about God's love.

Continue to call out colors until everyone has been to the center of the circle at least once. Then have the children sit in a circle. As you shake each child's hand, complete this sentence: (Child's name), **God has given you a great gift. You are a special person with special abilities. Use your gifts to work together with others for God.**

Then pray: **God, thank you for all of the gifts you give us. And thank you for the opportunity to share them with one another and to work together for you. Amen.**

**LEARNING LAB**

**THE POINT** ⭐

**...AND NEHEMIAH 7:**

God wants us to work together for him.

## KEY VERSE

*"God chose you to be his people, so I urge you now to live the life to which God called you"* (Ephesians 4:1b).

# GROWING TOGETHER

Permission to photocopy this handout from Group's Hands-On Bible Curriculum™ for Grades 1 and 2 granted for local church use. Copyright © Group Publishing, Inc., P.C. Box 481, Loveland, CO 80539.

## I·N T·O·U·C·H

Today your child learned that working together for God accomplishes great things, and it's fun, too. The children learned that God gives every follower special gifts and abilities to use to make the kingdom of God stronger. Use these ideas at home to teach your child how to have fun working with others.

## POPCORN TREATS

Have your family work together to make this sweet treat. Have someone pop popcorn; you'll need six quarts of popped corn. Have an adult mix 1 cup of corn syrup in a pan with a 3-ounce package of your favorite flavored gelatin and a cup of sugar and cook it on the stove until the sugar melts. Cool the syrup until it's barely comfortable to the touch, then pour it over the popcorn. Work together to form the popcorn into balls. Put the balls on wax paper. Enjoy the treat together.

## DEPENDENCE

Learn what it means to depend on each other. Have two family members sit about 18 inches apart with their backs toward each other, then have them lean back so their backs are touching. Have them relax completely so that all their weight is supported by the other person. Ask what would happen if one of the partners suddenly got up. Talk about how important it is to be able to depend on each other when you work together.

## SOLID WALL

With your child, collect 1-inch rocks. Place the rocks on a piece of plywood. Then mix a small amount of plaster of Paris and water in a plastic bucket according to the directions on the package. Quickly spread plaster on the rocks and build a vertical wall with them, using the plaster as a mortar. Work quickly so the plaster doesn't set before your wall is finished. Then read about Nehemiah's directing the work to rebuild the wall around Jerusalem in Nehemiah 3:1–4:23 and 6:1-15. Talk about the cooperation that was required to build both walls.

## ALL TOGETHER

Have all the members of your family hold hands as you take a walk through a park. Then read Ephesians 4:16. Talk about what it means to be joined together. Have everyone join hands again and have each person try to lead the family in a different direction. After a minute or two of struggle, sit down and talk about the need for common goals when you work together. Write a list of goals that your family can work toward. For example, you might set a goal of keeping the family room tidy for a week.

# K·I·N·D
# T·O A·L·L

*July 20—teach*

## THE POINT
God wants us to help people who are being treated unfairly.

It's important to say The Point just as it's written in each activity. Repeating The Point over and over will help children remember it and apply it to their lives.

## THE BIBLE BASIS:
Nehemiah 5:1-13. Nehemiah helps the poor.

The people of Jerusalem were in an economic crisis. Providing for their families had become so burdensome that many were borrowing money against their land and were selling their sons and daughters into slavery just to put food on the table. The wealthy leaders of the city were getting rich from the unfair interest they charged on loans to their less fortunate neighbors. Nehemiah was furious when he discovered this. He called down the wealthy citizens, demanding that they give back what they had taken. They listened to Nehemiah and promised to give back the fields, vineyards, olive groves, and houses they had taken.

Children treat others unfairly, too. First- and second-graders are starting to develop a social hierarchy. It's cool to own certain toys and to be interested in certain TV shows. Some kids don't fit in because of what they don't have or how they look. But first- and second-grade children are also developing a keen sense of justice—they recognize unfairness, especially when it happens to them. Use this lesson to make children sensitive to the unfairness that others suffer. Help them learn that they can stand up for people who are being treated unfairly.

Other Scriptures used in this lesson are Isaiah 58:10; Ezekiel 18:5, 9; and Amos 5:24.

## KEY VERSE
### for Lessons 6–9

*"God chose you to be his people, so I urge you now to live the life to which God called you"* (Ephesians 4:1b).

# GETTING THE POINT

Children will

- learn that they should always treat others fairly,
- see that they can do a lot to help others who are treated unfairly, and
- brush away each other's hurts as they learn that doing good makes them shine like the sun.

Before the lesson, collect the items from the Learning Lab for the activities you plan to use. Refer to the pictures in the margin to see what each item looks like.

# THIS LESSON AT A GLANCE

| SECTION | MINUTES | WHAT CHILDREN WILL DO | LEARNING LAB SUPPLIES | CLASSROOM SUPPLIES |
|---|---|---|---|---|
| WELCOME TIME | up to 5 | **Welcome!**—Receive a warm welcome from the teacher and make name tags. | | "Temple of God" name tags (p. 83), markers, scissors, tape |
| ATTENTION GRABBER | up to 10 | **Wounds and Hurts**—Talk about unfair treatment as they swing a ball at a spider web full of bugs. | Spider web, black insects, return ball | Tape |
| BIBLE EXPLORATION & APPLICATION | up to 13 | **Unfair Business**—Listen to the story from Nehemiah 5 about Nehemiah's standing up to unfair business practices. | Black insects | Bible |
| | up to 12 | **Rivers of Fairness**—Make pictures that illustrate the concept from Amos 5:24 that fairness should flow like a river. | Burlap | Bible, paper, glue, markers |
| | up to 10 | **Fair Situations**—Choose what they'd do to restore fairness or to act kindly to others who have been treated unfairly and learn from Ezekiel 18:5, 9 that those who are fair do right. | Big eraser | Bible, newsprint, tape, pencil  2x3ft. |
| CLOSING | up to 10 | **Brushed Away**—Brush away each other's hurts and learn that those who are kind to others will shine like the noonday sun. | Tinsel wand, paintbrushes | Bible |

Remember to make photocopies of the "Growing Together" handout (p. 104) to send home with your children. "Growing Together" is a valuable tool for helping first- and second-graders talk with their parents about what they're learning in class.

# T·H·E L·E·S·S·O·N

## ELCOME TIME

### WELCOME!
**(up to 5 minutes)**

- Greet each child individually with an enthusiastic smile.
- Thank each child for coming to class today.
- As children arrive, ask them about last week's "Growing Together" discussion. Use questions such as "How did your family work together last week?" and "What did you learn about working together?"
- Say: **Today we're going to learn that ★ God wants us to help people who are being treated unfairly.**
- Help children put on their name tags. If some children weren't in class last week, or if some of the name tags were damaged, photocopy the "Temple of God" name tags (p. 83) and have children follow the instructions to create new name tags.
- Tell the children that the attention-getting signal you'll use during this lesson is clapping your hands three times. Ask children to respond by clapping their hands three times as they stop talking and focus their attention on you. Rehearse the signal with the children, telling them to respond quickly so you have plenty of time for all the fun activities planned for this lesson.

**THE POINT** ★

## TTENTION GRABBER

**LEARNING LAB**

### WOUNDS AND HURTS
**(up to 10 minutes)**

Suspend the *spider web* from a doorway in your classroom. If you don't have a doorway, suspend it from the ceiling. Just a few small pieces of tape will hold it in place. Stretch out the web so that it fills the entire doorway from the top to the floor.

Gather the children around the doorway and give them each a *black insect*. Say: **Pretend this black bug is you. Find a home for the bug in the *spider web*.**

Have each child put his or her bug in the *spider web*. Make sure the bugs are spread out.

Say: **Today we're going to talk about things that are unfair. Think about the unfair things that have happened to you or that you've seen happen to other people. Each person will get a chance to tell about something that was unfair.** Hold up the *return ball*. **We'll throw this ball at the *spider web* for each unfair thing we can think of.**

Have the children sit 10 feet away from the *spider web* and take turns mentioning unfair things and throwing the *return ball* through the *spider web*. Make sure the children put the ball's ring around their fingers so they don't have to retrieve the ball.

After each child has had at least one turn, stop the game; remove the *spider web* from the doorway; and return it, the *black insects,* and the *return ball* to the Learning Lab. Then ask:

● **What happened to the bugs as the *return ball* kept going through the *spider web*?** (Some of them got hit by the ball; some fell.)

● **How is that like the way people feel when they've been treated unfairly?** (Being treated unfairly makes you feel like you've been hit; being treated unfairly hurts.)

Say: **No one likes to be treated unfairly. God doesn't like it either. We're going to find out what happened when Nehemiah learned about some people who were being treated unfairly. He knew that ✦ God wants us to help people who are being treated unfairly.**

 **THE POINT**

# **B** IBLE EXPLORATION & APPLICATION

## UNFAIR BUSINESS 📖

### (up to 13 minutes)

Open your Bible to Nehemiah 5. Have the children sit in a circle. Say: **Listen to this story from the book of Nehemiah.**

**Some of the people in Jerusalem were hurting, and they started to complain. They said, "We don't have enough food to feed our families. We can't grow enough food to eat, and we're borrowing money just to buy grain. The people who lend us money say that it's not enough for us to repay the money we borrowed. They make us give them our fields and our vineyards, too. It's just not fair! Other people are getting rich, and we just keep getting poorer and hungrier. And there's no way for us to make money in the future because we don't have land to grow crops anymore.**

**Then the people said, "We have to borrow money to pay our taxes to the king. We've already given up our land so we could buy food, and there's no money left to pay taxes. We've had to sell our sons and**

daughters into slavery to have enough money to give to the king. It's just not fair! The king is making money, and we have to sell our children.

**Let's see how this unfair business worked.**

Form groups of three. Give one child in each trio four black bugs. Give the second child two black bugs. Don't give the third child any black bugs.

Say: **Those of you with four bugs are the kings and queens of the land. You're already rich, but you demand that everyone else pay taxes to you. You've decided that the tax this year is to be one black bug. Collect one black bug from the other members of your trio.**

One child in each trio will be able to pay the tax. The other child won't have any bugs. Have the child without bugs borrow one from the child who has two bugs. Have them give their bugs to the king or queen of their trio.

Say: **Now the kings and queens are even richer. The one who loaned a bug to his friend decides that he wants his money back. If you loaned a bug to your friend, ask for it back. But don't ask for one bug; ask for two.**

Have the children demand that their friends repay their loans. Ask the children without any bugs:

● **What did you do, since you don't have any money to repay your friend?** (I didn't know what to do because I don't have any money; I was angry because I only borrowed one bug, so she shouldn't ask me to pay her back with two.)

Say: **That's just what was happening in Jerusalem. Some people were getting very rich. Others had to borrow money, and the people who loaned the money wanted more in return than they had loaned.** Collect all the bugs.

Then continue: **When Nehemiah heard what was happening, he was very angry. He gathered all of the wealthy people and the leaders and said, "You are being unfair. When you loan money to your friends and neighbors, you're asking them to pay you back much more than they borrowed."**

Nehemiah said, **"What you're doing is wrong. Don't you know that God isn't pleased with this? Stop asking for so much in return and give your neighbors back their fields so that they can grow food for their families. Also give them back the extra you've made them pay."**

**The wealthy people and the leaders realized that Nehemiah was right. They promised that they would stop taking things from their neighbors.**

**Nehemiah made sure he was fair and kind, too. He was the governor of the land. That meant that he could have demanded extravagant things from the people. But he didn't. Plus, he worked on the wall himself, and his servants fed many people every day. Nehemiah knew that the people were working hard to provide food for their families, so he was kind and didn't demand riches from them.** Ask:

● **How would you feel if you didn't have food to eat or if you didn't have enough money to pay for something?** (I'd feel awful; I'd feel like I needed a good friend.)

# BIBLE INSIGHT

Nehemiah was upset because Jewish leaders were lending large sums of money to poor people. When debtors missed a payment, the leaders took over the debtors' land and, often, their children. Nehemiah insisted that fairness to all is central to following God. Throughout the Bible, God shows us that caring for one another is more important than personal gain.

● **Have you ever borrowed money? What happened?** (Yes, I borrowed money from my mom to buy a new doll; yes, I borrowed money from my friend to buy a candy bar.)

● **Did you pay back just what you had borrowed, or did you have to pay back more?** (I paid back only what I'd borrowed; I didn't have to pay back more.)

● **How would you feel if your friends were as unfair to you as the wealthy people in this story were to their poor neighbors?** (Mad; sad; like I'd lost my friends.)

Say: **Nehemiah was upset because some people were being unfair to others. Some people were starving while other people were getting rich. Nehemiah stood up and told them not to be unfair anymore. Nehemiah pleased God because**  **God wants us to help people who are being treated unfairly.**

 **THE POINT**

# RIVERS OF FAIRNESS 📖

## (up to 12 minutes)

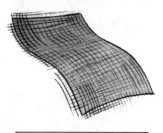
Before class, unravel what's left of the *burlap*.

During class set out paper, glue, markers, and the *burlap* strings.

Say: **Listen while I read from the Bible. Be ready to tell me what fairness and goodness are like.**

Read Amos 5:24, substituting the word "fairness" for "justice" so that it's easier for children to understand. If you'd rather use the word "justice," be sure to explain its meaning to the children. Ask:

● **What are fairness and goodness like?** (Like a river; like a stream that always flows.)

● **What does it mean that fairness should flow like a river?** (It means that there should be a lot of fairness; that it should never end.)

Say: **One thing it might mean is that we shouldn't be fair only when we feel like it, but we should be fair all the time, just as a river flows all the time. Let's make river pictures to remind us to be fair.**

Give each child some of the *burlap* strings and a sheet of paper. Have the children glue the *burlap* strings to the paper to create an ever-flowing river. Have them write "Let fairness flow like a river" on the pictures. If you have time, let children decorate the rest of the page to look like the banks of the river.

While children are working, have them discuss these questions with the children sitting next to them. Ask:

● **What can you do to be fair today?** (I can be nice to my little brother since I'm usually mean to him; I can give my cousin a big piece of cake.)

● **How can you help someone who is being treated unfairly?** (I can be friends with my neighbor who nobody likes; I can stand up for people who are being treated unfairly instead of teasing them.)

### Teacher Tip

If you have time, have the children join hands and play Follow the Leader. Lead the children around the classroom, imitating the meandering course of a river that always flows. Have the children chant, "Be fair like a river," as you walk around the room.

● Do you think it's possible to be fair all the time like a river that never stops flowing? Why or why not? (It might be possible if I were a really good person; it would be too hard for me.)

● What can you do to be fair more of the time? (I can remember what it feels like to be treated unfairly; I can remember to love others; I can remember to be like the river.)

When the pictures are finished, set them aside to dry. Say: **Being fair and helping others who are treated unfairly is important work. Take these pictures home to remind you to be fair all the time, like a river that always flows, because** ✸ **God wants us to help people who are being treated unfairly.**

# FAIR SITUATIONS 📖

## (up to 10 minutes)

Tape a piece of newsprint to the wall. Say: **Listen to what the Bible says about being fair.** Read Ezekiel 18:5, 9. Ask:

● **What do fair people do?** (They do right; they help others.)

Say: **Let's talk about some situations in which we need to decide what's fair. One of the things that fair people do is to help erase the hurts that other people have gone through. The first thing we'll do is to talk about the hurts that the people in these situations might have. I'll write the hurts on the newsprint with a pencil.**

**Then I'll put this eraser next to the newsprint. If you have an idea of how to help the people in these situations, you can come and pick up the eraser, tell your idea, and erase part of the hurt. Then we'll pass the eraser around until everyone who has an idea tells it. Here we go.**

Have the children sit on one side of the room. Read the situations aloud one by one. After you read each situation, ask:

● **What hurts might these people have?**

Write each hurt on the newsprint. Then, if children have ideas about how to help the people in the situations, have them come forward one by one and pick up the eraser. Have each child mention his or her idea and erase a few letters or a word from the newsprint.

After everyone has mentioned an idea, have the children sit down. Then read the next situation.

● **Situation #1: Your teacher gives stickers to the kids in your class when they've done a good job on their schoolwork. You find out that Jeff has been sneaking into the classroom and stealing stickers from other children. What could you do?**

● **Situation #2: A new girl has moved into town, and she's in your class. She has a funny-looking lunch box, and her clothes are funny-looking, too. Nobody talks to her very much, and some of the girls even giggle and make fun of her. What could you do to help her?**

**KEY VERSE** Connection

"God chose you to be his people, so I urge you now to live the life to which God called you" (Ephesians 4:1b).

God has chosen each of us to be his children. His judgment is always fair and right. In obedience to him, we should help those in need and encourage those who are treated unfairly by others.

● **Situation #3:** Your next-door neighbor lost his job, so his family has to be very careful not to spend too much money. They've decided to give up things like snacks and cable television to save money. Because the mom and dad are looking for jobs every day, the kids have to stay by themselves after school. What could you do to help?

After you've discussed all three situations, put away the *big eraser* and ask:

● **How was erasing the words like helping people who are hurting?** (When we help others, we make their hurts go away; when we help others, we're making things more fair.)

Say: **Unfair things happen every day. Sometimes people are unfair and unkind to each other like the girls who made fun of the new girl or the boy who stole stickers from other kids. Sometimes unfair things just happen like what happened to the parent who lost his job. No matter what kind of unfairness happens, we can help. We can do a lot to make others feel better and to stand up for others when people are unkind. Your ideas are super! God is pleased with your ideas because** ★ **God wants us to help people who are being treated unfairly.**

 **THE POINT**

W e believe Christian education extends beyond the classroom into the home. Photocopy the "Growing Together" handout (p. 104) for this week and send it home with your children. Encourage children and parents to use the handout to plan meaningful activities on this week's topic. Follow up the "Growing Together" activities next week by asking children what their families did.

*GROWING TOGETHER*

# CLOSING

## BRUSHED AWAY 📖

### (up to 10 minutes)

Ask:

● **What did you learn today?** (I learned that unfairness hurts me and others; I learned to stand up for others who are treated unfairly; I learned that I can help others.)

Say: **When we help others who are being treated unfairly, it's as if we are brushing their hurts away.**

Hand out the *paintbrushes* to volunteers. Give each *paintbrush* holder 30 seconds to brush the back of everyone else's hand.

Then have the children with the *paintbrushes* stand by you. Read Isaiah 58:10 to them. Then hold the *tinsel wand* over each of the *paintbrush* holders' heads in turn and gently wave the wand. Say: **May your light shine in the darkness, and may you be as bright as the noonday sun as you help those who are treated unfairly.**

Then choose more volunteers to use the *paintbrushes* to brush the others' hands. Affirm these volunteers with the *tinsel wand* as well.

Continue until every child has had a chance to brush away the others' hurts and has been affirmed with the *tinsel wand*. Then say: **We know that ✦ God wants us to help people who are being treated unfairly. Let's ask God for help.**

Pray: **God, thank you for being concerned about people who are treated unfairly. Help us be kind to them and help us show your love to them. Amen.**

**THE POINT** ✦

Permission to photocopy this handout from Group's Hands-On Bible Curriculum™ for Grades 1 and 2 granted for local church use. Copyright © Group Publishing, Inc., P.O. Box 481, Loveland, CO 80539.

**EZRA AND NEHEMIAH 8:**

**God wants us to help people who are being treated unfairly.**

## KEY VERSE

*"God chose you to be his people, so I urge you now to live the life to which God called you"* (Ephesians 4:1b).

# GROWING TOGETHER

## IN T·O·U·C·H

Today your child learned that many people are treated unfairly. The children also learned that God is displeased when people are treated unfairly and that God wants us to work to make things right. They discovered that there are many things they can do every day to help those who are wounded by unfairness. Use these ideas at home to help children recognize and stand against unfairness.

### RIVERS OF SYRUP

• • • • • • •

Remind your family to be on the side of fairness. Serve waffles or pancakes and syrup for breakfast. Have each family member hold the syrup bottle high above the food and recite Amos 5:24: "Let [fairness] flow like a river, and let goodness flow like a stream that never stops."

### FAIRNESS CAKE

• • • • • • • • • •

This simple poundcake can be called Fairness Cake because it's made up of one pound of each ingredient. Cream 1 pound of butter or margarine with 1 pound of powdered sugar until the mixture is smooth. Add 6 eggs, one at a time, and beat well. Stir in 3 cups of cake flour. This cake tastes great with these four ingredients, but you may want to add 1 teaspoon of vanilla or lemon flavoring as well. Pour the batter into a greased and floured angel food cake pan or a Bundt pan and bake at 350 degrees for 1 hour and 15 minutes.

## NOONDAY SUN

• • • • • • • • • • •

These flowers will remind you to shine like the noonday sun! Read Isaiah 58:10. Then cut six circles out of yellow construction paper. Make the circles about two inches bigger than a small paper plate. Stack the circles on top of a paper plate and push a metal paper fastener through the circles and the plate. Spread the metal prongs in back of the paper plate. Next, cut the edges of the yellow circles to look like petals. Rotate the circles and separate the flower petals so that you have a very full blossom. Glue sunflower seeds to the middle of the blossom, completely covering it. Mount your flower on a bright-blue construction paper background and hang it in a sunny window.

## NEWS OF UNFAIRNESS

• • • • • • • • • • •

Watch the news on TV together and look for instances in which people are treated unfairly. During the commercials, turn off the sound and talk about what could be done to make things right. You may want to videotape the news before your children watch so you can leave out segments that aren't appropriate for your children. Talk about what you think news broadcasts might be like if everyone obeyed God's laws and treated each other with fairness.

# L·I·V·E F·O·R
# G·O·D

July 27th

★

## THE POINT
We can decide
to live for God.

It's important to say The Point just as it's written in each
activity. Repeating The Point over and over will help children
remember it and apply it to their lives.

## THE BIBLE BASIS:
Nehemiah 8:1–10:39. The people agree to serve God.

At last, the temple was restored, and the wall protecting the city was complete and secure. Now it was time for the Jews to put their lives back in order.
They all gathered for a time of Scripture reading, confession, prayer, and worship—they were ready for a spiritual renewing. The people made a solemn commitment to follow God's laws. They wrote down their promises, and then the
men, women, sons, and daughters all took an oath to observe the laws of God.

First- and second-graders are learning that their actions have consequences and that they can make decisions that will affect
how their lives will turn out. Every day children make
choices about how to behave and how to interact
with God and others. Every day they can
decide to live for God. Use this lesson to help
children see that their most important decisions will be about following God. Help children learn that they can promise to follow
God, just as the Jews did in this passage from
Nehemiah.

Other Scriptures used in this lesson are
Psalm 20:5b; 2 Timothy 4:7-8; and 1 John 5:3-4.

## KEY VERSE
for Lessons 6–9

"God chose you to be his
people, so I urge you now to
live the life to which God
called you"
(Ephesians 4:1b).

# GETTING THE POINT

Children will

- see that they can make decisions to live for God every day,
- understand that there are rewards for living for God, and
- sing praises to God.

Before the lesson, collect the items from the Learning Lab for the activities you plan to use. Refer to the pictures in the margin to see what each item looks like.

## THIS LESSON AT A GLANCE

| SECTION | MINUTES | WHAT CHILDREN WILL DO | LEARNING LAB SUPPLIES | CLASSROOM SUPPLIES |
|---|---|---|---|---|
| WELCOME TIME | up to 5 | **Welcome!**—Receive a warm welcome from the teacher and make name tags. | | "Temple of God" name tags (p. 83), markers, scissors, tape |
| ATTENTION GRABBER | up to 12 | **Flags for God**—Create flags that show what God is like and learn about being loyal to God. | Paint set, paint-brushes, foam shapes, jump-rope or lariat | Construction paper, crayons, markers, tape |
| BIBLE EXPLORATION & APPLICATION | up to 13 | **Living for God**—Learn about how Ezra read God's Word to the Jews and how they listened and agreed to live for God. | | Bibles |
| | up to 10 | **Scrolls**—Turn their flags into scrolls that show they are choosing to obey God in accordance with 1 John 5:3-4. | Black insects | Bible, flags from "Flags for God" activity, pencils, tape |
| | up to 10 | **Decisions**—Play a game that shows they make lots of decisions to live for God, read 2 Timothy 4:7-8, and receive crowns for running the race. | Visor, tinsel wand | Bible |
| CLOSING | up to 10 | **Song Praises**—Sing praises to God to show they want to live for God. | Cassette: "Praise Ye the Lord," "Lyrics Poster" | Cassette player, flags from "Flags for God" activity |

Remember to make photocopies of the "Growing Together" handout (p. 113) to send home with your children. "Growing Together" is a valuable tool for helping first- and second-graders talk with their parents about what they're learning in class.

# T·H·E L·E·S·S·O·N

## **W**ELCOME TIME

### WELCOME!
**(up to 5 minutes)**

- Greet each child individually with an enthusiastic smile.
- Thank each child for coming to class today.
- As children arrive, ask them about last week's "Growing Together" discussion. Use questions such as "What did your family make to learn about fairness?" and "What did you see that was unfair on the news?"
- Say: **Today we're going to learn that** ✦ **we can decide to live for God.**
- Help children put on their name tags. If some children weren't in class last week, or if some of the name tags were damaged, photocopy the "Temple of God" name tags (p. 83) and have children follow the instructions to create new name tags.
- Tell the children that the attention-getting signal you'll use during this lesson is clapping your hands three times. Ask children to respond by clapping their hands three times as they stop talking and focus their attention on you. Rehearse the signal with the children, telling them to respond quickly so you have plenty of time for all the fun activities planned for this lesson.

**THE POINT** ★

## **A**TTENTION GRABBER

**LEARNING LAB**

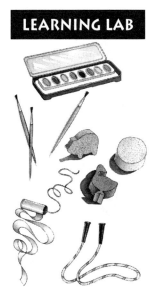

### FLAGS FOR GOD 📖
**(up to 12 minutes)**

Say: **One of the ways that people show what side they're on is to fly a flag. For example, we fly our nation's flag on the Fourth of July. A long time ago, pirates flew pirate flags from their ships. And in a war, warriors knew which way to go by following the flags of their countries. Psalm 20:5 says, "We will raise a flag in the name of our God." Let's make flags to show that we're on God's team.**

Set out construction paper, crayons, markers, water, and the *paint set, paintbrushes,* and *foam shapes.* Have the children design flags to show that they're on God's team. Children might draw a rock to show that God is their strength or a sheep to show that God is a shepherd. While the children are working, have them tell each other what the symbols mean. Have the children each use a whole sheet of paper to make their flags.

Tape the short end of the flags to the *jump-rope* or to the streamer of the *lariat*. Then use tape to hang the *jump-rope* or the *lariat* on your classroom wall. Gather the children where they can see all of the flags. Ask:

● **What do our flags tell us about God?** (They show that God is strong; God is good; God loves us; God is fair.)

Say: **From what our flags show, God is worthy of a lot of loyalty.** Ask:

● **What is loyalty?** (Loyalty means that you stick by someone; it means that you care about someone; it means that you're a good friend.)

Say: **Today we're talking about being loyal to God. We've made flags to show we're on God's team.** Ask:

● **What else can we do to be loyal to God?** (We can obey him; we can put God first; we can love God.)

Say: **Every day we make lots of choices. We decide what to wear, what to eat, what to say, who to be nice to, and what to do for fun. Today we're going to talk about the decisions we make about God. We're going to learn how to live for God. Every day ✪ we can decide to live for God. Let's find out what happened to Nehemiah and the people of Jerusalem when they decided to live for God.**

Return the *paint set, paintbrushes,* and *foam shapes* to the Learning Lab.

**THE POINT**

# BIBLE EXPLORATION & APPLICATION

## LIVING FOR GOD 📖

### (up to 13 minutes)

Have the children sit in a circle. Say: **Before we begin the Bible story, let's find all of the Bibles in this room.**

Have the children search the room for Bibles and bring them to the circle. If you know that only one Bible is in your classroom, take your children on a quick and silent walk through the halls of your church. Peek into the other classes and count Bibles.

When the Bibles have been counted, open your Bible to Nehemiah 8:1–10:39. Say: **We found several Bibles, but when our Bible story took place, only one person had a Bible. His name was Ezra. Since God's Word is so important, every time I say "God's Word" during our story, stand up and sit back down. Be silent to show respect for God's Word.**

**After the wall around Jerusalem was finished, the people of Israel**

gathered to listen to Ezra read from God's Word. (Pause.)

Men and women and everyone else who could understand listened carefully as Ezra read. He stood on a high platform and read loudly so that everyone could hear. The people were very quiet so that they could hear what he read.

When Ezra opened God's Word (pause), the people stood. He read from early morning until noon. Ezra praised God, and all the people said "amen" and worshiped God. Ask:

● **How do you think the people felt after they stood listening to God's Word?** (They were probably tired; I think they were listening so hard that they didn't mind standing up.)

Say: **Then other religious leaders helped explain what Ezra had read to be sure the people understood it. The people started to cry when they heard God's Word.** (Pause.) Ask:

● **Why do you think the people cried?** (Because they knew they had done wrong; because they were so happy to hear God's Word.)

Say: **The leaders said, "This is a happy day. Don't cry. Go and enjoy good food. The joy of the Lord will make you strong." So the people celebrated, and many came back the next day for more teaching.** Ask:

● **Why do you think they celebrated?** (I think they celebrated the good news of the Bible; I think they celebrated because they were happy to worship God.)

● **Why do you think they came back the next day for more teaching?** (Because they liked learning about God; because they wanted to know more.)

Say: **The next day, Ezra read from God's Word** (pause) **about a celebration called the Feast of Tabernacles. When the people heard what they were to do during that feast, they immediately obeyed. They built small shelters and lived in them for several days. Each day they celebrated and read more from God's Word.** (Pause.)

As Ezra read, the people began to understand the wrongs they had done. They confessed their sins to God and asked for forgiveness.

Then they wrote down a promise to live for God. They promised to obey God, to take care of the temple, and to care for the people who worked there. They had decided to live for God. Ask:

● **What do you think they learned about God that made them decide to live for God?** (I think they learned about how much God loves them; I think they learned about how God had taken care of them.)

● **Why do you live for God?** (My parents want me to live for God; my friends at church live for God; I know it's the right thing to do; I want to live for God because God loves me.)

Say: **When the people heard about how they had sinned and about how God cares for his people, they wanted to obey him and live for him. They promised to live for God.** ✦ **We can decide to live for God, too.**

## THE POINT ★

 **THE POINT**

# SCROLLS 📖
## (up to 10 minutes)

Say: **When Nehemiah and the people of Jerusalem heard what Ezra read from the scroll that contained God's Word, they knew they needed to obey God. Let's turn our flags into scrolls that show how we can obey God.**

Take the flags off of the *jump-rope* or the *lariat's* streamer. Have children each write on the blank side of their flags one thing they promise to do to obey God. They might write that they'll obey their parents, that they'll help people who are treated unfairly, that they'll put God first, or that they'll work together for God. Be ready to help with spelling.

When the children are finished writing, give each one two pencils. Have the children tape the pencils to the outside edges of their papers and roll them like scrolls.

Say: **Listen to what the Bible says about obeying God.** Read 1 John 5:3-4. Ask:

● **What does it mean to love God?** (It means to obey God; to pay attention to his commandments.)

● **How can you decide to live for God?** (I can decide to do what God wants; I can decide to follow God; I can decide to put God first.)

Say: **Let's find out how we can conquer the world by obeying God.**

Spread the *black insects* on a table top. Say: **Let's pretend that these black bugs are things that try to keep us from obeying God.** Ask:

● **What keeps us from obeying God?** (Sometimes friends at school say it's not cool to obey God; temptations.)

● **How can we win over those who want us to disobey God?** (We can just obey no matter what anyone else says; we can tell them it really is cool to obey God; we can ignore temptations.)

Say: **We can conquer all of these temptations with our decisions to obey God. Since we've written down our decisions on these scrolls, let's use our scrolls to conquer the world.**

Have the children swat the *black insects* off the table with the rolled-up scrolls. Ask:

● **How does it feel to swat all of these bugs away and to conquer the world?** (It feels great; it's fun.)

Say: ✦ **We can decide to live for God. Each of you is a champion because you've heard God's Word and you've made a decision to obey it. When we obey God, we have conquered the world. Let's find out what will happen to people who decide to live for God.**

Put the *black insects* and *jump-rope* or *lariat* away.

# DECISIONS 📖

## (up to 10 minutes)

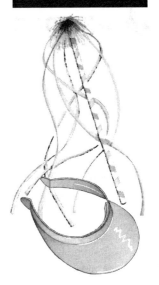

Say: **We can decide to live for God every day. Sometimes we make big decisions about living for God; for example, some of us might decide to become ministers or missionaries. That's a big decision because it takes a lot of preparation and study to be a minister or missionary. Other decisions might be smaller; for example, you might decide to smile at someone who's having a bad day. That's an action that pleases God. When you decide to do something that pleases God, you're deciding to live for God. Let's have fun with some of the decisions we can make that show we are living for God.**

Have the children stand up. Read the following statements, pausing after each one to give the children a chance to follow the instructions. Say:

● **If you've ever been kind to anyone, run in place for 30 seconds.**

● **If you've ever stood up for someone who was treated unfairly, punch the air in front of you five times.**

● **If you've ever listened to a Bible story, jump up and down 10 times.**

● **If you've ever sung a song to God, do 15 jumping jacks.**

● **If you've ever obeyed one of God's commands, hop on your left foot five times, then hop on your right foot five times.**

● **If you've ever had fun praising God, run in place for 30 seconds.**

Encourage the children to move quickly during this game. They should be out of breath by the end. Say: **All of you moved fast to show that you're making decisions to live for God. You're all out of breath. There are many more things we can do to show that we have decided to live for God. Think of how out of breath you'd be if we listed all of the decisions you make for God!** Ask:

● **What do you think about all the things you can do to live for God?** (There are a lot of them; it makes me tired to do all of that; I can make decisions for God all day long, every day.)

● **Do you get as tired living for God as you did during this game?** (Yes, because sometimes living for God is hard work; no, because it doesn't happen as fast as it did in this game.)

Say: **Living for God is like running a race. Listen to what the Bible says about running a race. Be ready to tell me what people who run the race will get.** Read 2 Timothy 4:7-8. Ask:

● **What will people who run the race get?** (A crown.)

Say: **Each of you will receive a crown today for being good runners in the race to live for God.**

Have the children sit in a semicircle. One by one, have the children come forward and sit by you in front of the semicircle. Put the *visor* on each child's head so that the bill stands straight up in the air.

Wave the *tinsel wand* gently over the child's head, and say: (Child's name), **you have been given the crown for running the race and for being right** with God. You've chosen to live for God by... May God send blessings to you as you decide to live for him. Use phrases such as "being kind to your classmates" or "respecting your teacher" to complete the middle sentence. Have the other children mention more ways that the child with the crown has decided to live for God.

Continue in this manner until every child has been affirmed.

**THE POINT**

Then say: ⭐ **We can decide to live for God every day. Let's do one more activity to show that we've made our decision.**

Return the *visor* and *tinsel wand* to the Learning Lab.

---

**W**e believe Christian education extends beyond the classroom into the home. Photocopy the "Growing Together" handout (p. 113) for this week and send it home with your children. Encourage children and parents to use the handout to plan meaningful activities on this week's topic. Follow up the "Growing Together" activities next week by asking children what their families did.

**GROWING TOGETHER**

---

# **C**LOSING

## SONG PRAISES
### (up to 10 minutes)

Ask:

● **What did you learn today?** (I learned that there are lots of things I can do to live for God; I learned to decide to live for God.)

Say: **One thing we can do to live for God is to praise God. Let's do that now with a song.**

Cue the *cassette tape* to "Praise Ye the Lord" and post the "Lyrics Poster" at the children's eye level. Give children their scrolls and have them open the scrolls and turn them over to show their flags. Have the children hold up their flags as they sing "lift his praises high" and "praise Jehovah in the heights."

**THE POINT**

After the song, pray: **God, thank you for giving us the choice to praise you and to live for you. ⭐ We can decide to live for you every day. Help us to make good decisions and to praise you. We want to lift your flag for all the people to see. Amen.**

**EZRA AND NEHEMIAH 9:**

**We can decide to live for God.**

## KEY VERSE

*"God chose you to be his people, so I urge you now to live the life to which God called you"* *(Ephesians 4:1b).*

# GROWING TOGETHER

## I·N T·O·U·C·H

Today your child learned that he or she can make decisions to live for God every day. The children learned that each time they decide to be kind, to be fair, or to praise God, they're choosing to live for God. Help your child live for God this week with these activities.

## BEAUTIFUL LIVES

Pry off the top of an empty roll-on deodorant container or take the sponge-applicator top off of a bottle of shoe polish. Wash the container and applicator thoroughly. Then refill the bottle with thin tempera paint and replace the applicator. Have your child use the newly filled bottle to create a beautiful picture. Talk about how God fills us up with new and beautiful things when we decide to live for him.

## REFLECTING GOD

Cut out a panel of an empty cereal box. Then cut shapes from aluminum foil and glue them to the blank side of the cardboard panel. When the glue has dried, hold the panel so that the foil is facing the sun or a bright light. Move the panel around so you can see the reflection against the ceiling or wall. Talk about how we reflect God's goodness when we decide to live for him.

## FOLLOWING FOOTSTEPS

Have your child trace his or her footprint on several sheets of construction paper. Then cut out the footprints. When your child makes a specific decision to do something that shows that he or she is living for  God, have him or her write about it on one of the footprints. For example, your child might write that a friend has tempted him or her to cheat on a test but your child resisted the temptation. Post the footprint on a wall or bulletin board or save it in a scrapbook to chronicle your child's journey with God.

## DECISIONS, DECISIONS

Involve your child in decision making at home. You might give your child several nutritious options for dinner and let him or her decide. Or your child might decide what to do for family fun-night. Your child could also choose to donate a portion of his or her allowance to a charity. Talk to your child about the responsibility that goes with decision making. Be sure to say that choosing to live for God is the most important decision we can make.

# S·C·H·O·O·L

The years spent in school will be some of the most exciting years in your students' lives. In school, your students will meet friends; some of them will become lifelong friends. They'll find out about places, people, and ideas they never knew existed. And they'll learn skills that will open doors to challenging and fulfilling futures. The eager and enthusiastic children who are in your classroom every week are learning every day.

The book of Proverbs teaches that knowledge begins with respect for God. You can help children begin to develop respect for God with the lessons in this module. From the examples of Solomon; the servant girl in Naaman's home; Daniel; and Shadrach, Meshach, and Abednego, the children in your class will learn principles that will help them please God and learn well during their years in school. The children will learn to please God by doing their best, by caring for others, and by telling the truth. And they'll learn to be diligent at school because learning is important to God. Have fun preparing your students for a lifetime of learning.

## FOUR LESSONS ON SCHOOL

| LESSON | PAGE | THE POINT | THE BIBLE BASIS |
|---|---|---|---|
| 10—DO YOUR BEST | 119 | God is pleased when we do our best. | 1 Kings 3:3-15; 4:29-34 |
| 11—CARE FOR OTHERS | 131 | God is pleased when we care about others. | 2 Kings 5:1-14 |
| 12—COME AND LEARN! | 141 | Learning is important to God. | Daniel 1:3-20 |
| 13—TELL THE TRUTH | 149 | God is pleased when we tell the truth. | Daniel 3:1-30 |

# THE SIGNAL

During the lessons on school, your attention-getting signal will be clapping your hands three times. Have children respond by clapping their hands three times as they stop talking and focus their attention on you. Tell children about this signal before the lesson begins. Explain that it's important to respond to this signal quickly so the class can do as many fun activities as possible.

# THE FIDGET BUSTER

If children are too antsy to pay attention to the lesson, use this fidget buster to help them get the wiggles out.

Have the children stand far enough apart from each other to allow them to move freely.

Say: **When I say "add," start with your fists down low and put one fist on top of the other, again and again, until your fists are high in the air.** Have the children do this action with you.

Say: **When I say "subtract," start with your fists up in the air and put one fist under the other, again and again, until your fists are low to the ground.** Have the children do this action with you.

Say: **When I say "alphabet," say the alphabet as quickly as you can.** Have the children say the alphabet.

Say: **When I say, "lunch time," sit on the floor and pretend to eat.** Have the children do this action.

Say: **When I say "recess," stand in place and pretend to play your favorite outside game.** Have the children do this action.

Say: **When I say, "You're late for school," run in place.** Have the children do this action.

Call out "add," "subtract," "alphabet," "lunch time," "recess," and "You're late for school" in random order for several minutes. Then call out: **Now it's time to move on in our class.** Return to your lesson.

# THE TIME STUFFER

The children will create a mural for this module's Time Stuffer.

Hang several sheets of newsprint on a wall to create a square. Draw the outline of a head that fills up most of the space on the newsprint. Refer to the drawing in the margin.

At the top of the mural, print these words from Job 34:4b: "Let's learn together what is good."

Place scissors, markers, tape, and a stack of construction paper near the mural.

When children arrive in class early or finish a project before others do, have them use the construction paper to cut out shapes representing what they think they'll learn in school this year. Have them tape their shapes inside the outline of the head to show what their minds will be filled with. The children might cut out numbers, letters, or words they think they'll learn about. They might also cut out animal shapes or the shapes of countries or people that they think they might learn about.

# EMEMBERING GOD'S WORD

Key verse: "Always remember what you have been taught, and don't let go of it. Keep all that you have learned; it is the most important thing in life" (Proverbs 4:13).

This module's key verse will remind children of the value of learning. Use these activities any time during the lessons on school.

# HOLDING ON

Choose one child to be "It." Give all the children except It either a *foam shape* or a piece of *plastic foam*. Say: **Pretend that the foam piece is an important treasure and hold on to it tightly. Do your best to keep from being tagged by It. If you're tagged, give your foam piece to It. Then you become It, and it's your turn to try to tag someone.**

Play the game for several minutes, making sure that many children have a turn at being It. Then put the *foam shapes* and pieces of *plastic foam* on the floor and gather the children in a circle around them. Ask:

● **What was it like to try to hold on to your important possession?** (It was fun; it was hard because I kept getting tagged; I was excited.)

● **How did you feel when you were tagged and had to give up your possession?** (I felt awful; I felt like I'd done a bad thing; I knew I had to try hard to get another one.)

● **What's your most important possession?** (My rock collection; my Barbie doll; my catcher's mitt; my Bible.)

● **What would you do if you had to give it away?** (I'd be mad; I'd cry; I'd hide it so no one could find it; I'd fight before I gave it away.)

● **What do you do with your most important possession to make sure nothing happens to it?** (I keep it in a secret place; I take care of it; I make sure that it's in a safe place where it won't get broken.)

Say: **Listen to what the Bible says about an important possession.** Read Proverbs 4:13. Ask:

● **Why is knowledge so important?** (Because knowing things helps us live better; knowledge keeps us out of trouble; knowing things will help us get good jobs; knowing about God makes us better Christians.)

● **What are some things you have learned that you don't want to forget?** (Where I live; how to do subtraction; how to read; how to tie my shoes.)

● **What might happen if you forgot something important?** (I might fail a test in school; I'd be lost because I wouldn't be able to remember how to get home.)

● **How can you hold on to knowledge?** (By studying hard; by doing lots of math so I remember how to do it.)

Say: **The things we learn help us all the time. We learn our addresses and phone numbers in case we get lost. We learn how to read so we can read signs and newspapers and books. We learn how to operate computers and telephones and other machines so that we can live in the world. God's Word says that it's important to hold on to what we learn—to remember it and use it. Think of the trouble we could get in if we forgot where we lived or if we forgot how to read.**

**Let's say the verse together to help us remember that learning is important to God.**

Say Proverbs 4:13 in sections and have the children repeat each section after you. Then say the verse all together.

# FORGOTTEN KNOWLEDGE

Help children each write on a slip of paper one thing they've learned that they don't want to forget.

Put all of the slips of paper into the lid of the Learning Lab box. Form pairs and have each pair pick out one slip of paper.

Give the pairs five minutes to think of skits about what life would be like if they forgot how to do what is written on the slips of paper they chose.

Have each pair perform its skit for the rest of the class. If you have time, have each pair choose another slip of paper and prepare a second skit.

After all the skits have been performed, have the children sit on the floor. Ask:

● **What would it be like if you really forgot how to do these things?** (It would be terrible; I'd be lost all the time; I'd never get to the next grade in school.)

● **What kinds of things do we tend to forget in real life?** (I forget to do my chores; sometimes I forget vocabulary words; during summer vacation, I forgot the things I learned at school last year.)

● **How do you remember the things that are important to remember?** (I say them over and over in my mind; I study hard; I do my homework; I practice; my mom helps me remember some things.)

Say: **Listen to this Bible verse about remembering.** Read Proverbs 4:13. Ask:

● **Why is knowledge important?** (Because things get messed up when people forget; because God says it's important; because knowing things helps a person get a good job.)

● **What would life be like if we forgot everything we learned?** (We'd be lost; we wouldn't know how to do important things.)

Say: **Knowledge is important every day. We need to remember how to tie our shoes, how to get to school, how to do math, and how to read. We also need to remember how to please God. Let's say the verse to help us remember that knowledge is important.**

Say Proverbs 4:13 together.

# D·O  Y·O·U·R
# B·E·S·T

*Aug. 3rd–*
*teach*

## THE POINT
God is pleased
when we do our
best.

It's important to say The Point just as it's written in each
activity. Repeating The Point over and over will help children
remember it and apply it to their lives.

## THE BIBLE BASIS:
1 Kings 3:3-15; 4:29-34. Solomon asks for wisdom.

Near the beginning of Solomon's reign as the king of Israel, he went to
Gibeon to worship. God appeared to Solomon in a dream and said, "Ask for whatever you want me to give you." Solomon could have asked for a long life or great
riches. But Solomon had discovered that ruling a country was tough, so he asked
for wisdom and an obedient heart. God was pleased with Solomon's request and
gave Solomon wisdom and understanding. Solomon used his wisdom to rule fairly and to help the nation follow God. Thousands of years later, we benefit from
God's gift to Solomon. Much of his wisdom is recorded in Proverbs.

Solomon knew he needed God's help to do his best. First-
and second-graders need God's help, too. They're beginning their school careers, and in the next 10 to 15
years they'll be challenged intellectually, socially,
emotionally, and spiritually. God expects us to
try our best to serve him and to serve each
other. But God also promises to give us all
the help we need to reach the goals he has
for us. Use this lesson to help your students strive
to do their best in everything.

Other Scriptures used in this lesson are Philippians 4:13; Hebrews 6:11;
10:24-25; and James 1:5.

## KEY VERSE
### for Lessons 10–13

"Always remember what
you have been taught, and
don't let go of it. Keep all
that you have learned; it is
the most important thing
in life"
(Proverbs 4:13).

# GETTING THE POINT

Children will

● discover that doing their best takes patience and persistence,

● see that God promises to help them do their best, and

● encourage one another to do things well.

Before the lesson, collect the items from the Learning Lab for the activities you plan to use. Refer to the pictures in the margin to see what each item looks like.

## THIS LESSON AT A GLANCE

| SECTION | MINUTES | WHAT CHILDREN WILL DO | LEARNING LAB SUPPLIES | CLASSROOM SUPPLIES |
|---------|---------|----------------------|----------------------|--------------------|
| WELCOME TIME | up to 5 | **Welcome!**—Receive a warm welcome from the teacher and make name tags. | | "Schoolhouse Name Tags" (p. 128), markers, scissors, tape |
| ATTENTION GRABBER | up to 10 | **Forever Actions**—Continue to do the same action for a full minute, then talk about how hard it is to do their best for a long time. | | |
| BIBLE EXPLORATION & APPLICATION | up to 13 📖 | **Solomon's Request**—Listen to the story from 1 Kings 3:3-15; 4:29-34 about Solomon's asking God for wisdom and learn that they can ask God for wisdom to help them do their best. | Tinsel wand | Bible |
| | up to 10 📖 | **Persistence**—Be persistent in stretching the spider web across the room, read Hebrews 6:11, and learn that God wants them to work hard at doing their best all the time. | Spider web | Bible |
| | up to 12 📖 | **God's Strength**—Play a tossing game, read Philippians 4:13, and see that God strengthens them to do their best. | Plastic foam, big eraser, black insects | Bible, masking tape, transparent tape |
| CLOSING | up to 10 📖 | **Encouragements**—Listen to Hebrews 10:24-25 and encourage each other to do their best. | Rainbow shark | Bible |

Remember to make photocopies of the "Growing Together" handout (p. 129) to send home with your children. "Growing Together" is a valuable tool for helping first- and second-graders talk with their parents about what they're learning in class.

# T·H·E L·E·S·S·O·N

##  ELCOME TIME

### WELCOME!
**(up to 5 minutes)**

- Greet each child individually with an enthusiastic smile.
- Thank each child for coming to class today.
- As children arrive, ask them about last week's "Growing Together" discussion. Use questions such as "How did you live for God last week?" and "What did you learn about decision making?"
- Say: **Today we're going to learn that**  **God is pleased when we do our best.**
- Help children make name tags. Photocopy the "Schoolhouse Name Tags" (p. 128) and follow the instructions.
- Tell the children that the attention-getting signal you'll use during this lesson is clapping your hands three times. Ask children to respond by clapping their hands three times as they stop talking and focus their attention on you. Rehearse the signal with the children, telling them to respond quickly so you have plenty of time for all the fun activities planned for this lesson.

**THE POINT** ✦

## ATTENTION GRABBER

### FOREVER ACTIONS
**(up to 10 minutes)**

Have the children stand in a circle. Tell each child to do a specific action. For example, you might tell one child to pat his head while another child counts out loud while yet another child snaps her fingers. Assign a different action to each child.

Say: **Continue doing this action until I clap three times.**

Sit quietly for a full 60 seconds. If the children don't seem to be wondering why they're doing these actions, extend the time to 90 seconds.

Call time by clapping your hands three times. Wait for the children to respond by clapping three times and focusing their attention on you. Then ask:

- **How did you like this activity?** (It was fun at first; I got tired of it; I wondered why we had to keep doing it; I got bored.)

● **Have you ever had to do a job that you had to keep doing even though it was tiring or boring? Tell us about it.** (Yes, I had to keep raking leaves until the whole yard was clean; yes, I had to clean my room when it was really messy, and it took all day.)

● **What do you do when you get tired of a job?** (I slow way down; I stop working; I find an excuse to do something else.)

Say: **These actions were kind of silly. You'll probably never again have to pat your head for that long. Just as we grew tired of doing these silly actions, sometimes we get tired of doing our best in our work at home and at school. Today we're going to talk about a man who was very important. In fact, he was a king. He knew that ✷ God is pleased when we do our best. Let's learn what he did that helped him to do his best.**

### ★ THE POINT

# BIBLE EXPLORATION & APPLICATION

## SOLOMON'S REQUEST  📖

**(up to 13 minutes)**

**LEARNING LAB**

Open your Bible to 1 Kings 3:3-15; 4:29-34.

Say: **Since we're talking about doing our best today, think of an action that represents you doing your best. Maybe you want to do your best to learn math. Your action could be drawing a plus sign and a minus sign in the air with your finger.** Ask:

● **In what area do you want to do your best?** (Math; reading; cooking; playing the piano.)

● **What will your action be?** (Drawing a plus sign; writing in the air; stirring a pot; pretending to play the piano.)

Say: **Solomon was the king of Israel, and he wanted to do his best. Each time I mention his name, do your action to show that you want to do your best, too. Let's practice. Solomon.** Have each child do an action. **Great! Now let's tell the story.**

Say: **Solomon** (pause) **found out that being a king is hard work. There's always a lot to do.** Ask:

● **What do you think a king might have to do?** (Make laws; punish criminals; have meetings with other kings.)

Say: **Solomon** (pause) **worked hard to do all these things. He made fair laws and settled disagreements between people. He also worked hard to follow God and to see that the entire country followed God. Solomon** (pause) **wanted to do his best.**

One day, Solomon (pause) **went to worship at a place called Gibeon (GIB-ee-uhn). While he was there, God appeared to Solomon** (pause) **in a dream and said, "Ask for whatever you want me to give you."** Ask:

● **If God said to you, "Ask for whatever you want," what would you ask for?** (A lot of money; for my mom and dad to stay married; for my sisters to leave me alone; for eternal life.)

Say: **Solomon** (pause) **said, "You were kind to my father, David. My father obeyed you—he was honest, and he lived right. You showed him a great kindness when you allowed me, David's son, to be king after him.**

**"God, I am just like a young child. I haven't learned everything I need to know to be a good king. Help me to obey you, so that I can rule the people the right way. Also help me know the difference between right and wrong so that I can do my best to be a good king. I need your help; otherwise, it will be impossible for me to rule your people."**

**God was pleased that Solomon** (pause) **had asked for wisdom. God said, "Solomon,** (pause) **you could have asked for a long life or for a lot of money, but you didn't. You asked for wisdom to make the right decisions so that you can be a good and wise king. I will give you what you asked. You will have wisdom and understanding that is greater than anyone else has ever had.**

**"And because you have pleased me, I'll also give you riches and honor even though you didn't ask for them. No king will be as great as you. If you follow me, I'll give you a long life, too."**

**Then Solomon** (pause) **woke up from his dream. He worshiped God and gave a great feast to celebrate.**

**Solomon** (pause) **became wiser than anyone else. He said many wise things that are written in the Bible. People from many nations came to listen to him because he was so wise.**

**Because Solomon** (pause) **had asked for wisdom, he was able to do his best in ruling the kingdom.**

**Now, listen to this verse from the Bible. Be ready to tell me what can help you do your best.**

Read James 1:5. Then ask:

● **What do you think you can do to help you do your best?** (Ask God for help; ask God for wisdom.)

Say: **Solomon's job was to be a good king, and he wanted to do the best job he could. Soon, your job will be to go back to school and be a good student.** Ask:

● **What do you need to be a good student?** (Patience; wisdom; I need to listen better; I need help paying attention.)

Say: **Let's ask God to help us be good students. Since we really shine when we do our best, let's use the shiny *tinsel wand* as we pray. Each of you will get a chance to wrap the strands of tinsel around the wand. Pray, "God help me do my best to . . ." and complete the sentence with how you'd like God to help you be a good student. Then watch as you release the tinsel and it falls gracefully downward. That will show that God**

# BIBLE INSIGHT

One of the major achievements of Solomon's reign was the completion of construction of the temple, which had begun during the reign of his father, David. As the final touch, the ark of the covenant was brought from David's Tabernacle to the temple in a great parade. Solomon spoke the dedicatory prayer and sermon at the ceremony. In this manner, he was divinely confirmed and recognized before his own nation as the ruler over God's own people.

will give us what we need, just as he promises.

Give each child a chance to pray and use the *tinsel wand*. Then put the wand away and say: **We know that God answers our prayers.** ✦ **God is pleased when we do our best. God gave Solomon the wisdom he needed to do his best at being king. God will give us what we need to do our best at our jobs, too.**

# PERSISTENCE 📖
## (up to 10 minutes)

Say: **Let's do our best to stretch the *spider web* across the room.**

Gather children in the middle of the room and have them stand around the *spider web*. Have each child pull and stretch the *spider web* so that it is spread over the entire room. This will take several minutes. Some children will need to leave the edge of the web and position themselves underneath it to pull and stretch it from the middle of the room.

Point out where the fibers of the web are bunched up and direct some children to stretch out the bunches. Encourage the children to be patient and to keep trying.

Once the web is spread out, have the class celebrate its accomplishment with a round of applause. Then put the *spider web* away and ask:

● **What did you think as we were spreading out the *spider web?*** (It was too hard; I didn't think we'd ever get it done.)

● **What do you think now that you see what a great job we did?** (I'm proud that we kept working at it; I'm glad we didn't give up; I feel good that we did a good job.)

Say: **Listen to this Bible verse. Think about the work we've just done and the work we need to do in our everyday lives.** Read Hebrews 6:11. Ask:

● **What hard work do you need to keep doing?** (My chores at home; learning to read; being kind to my neighbors.)

Say: **Sometimes it's tough to keep on working and doing our best. Remember how tiny the *spider web* was when it was all bunched up. We worked hard to spread it out so that it filled the entire room. It was a big project, but each of you kept working until it was finished.** Ask:

● **What kinds of big projects do you work on?** (Cleaning the garage; homework.)

● **What makes a big project tough?** (It takes a long time to finish; it takes hard work; you have to keep going even when you're tired.)

● **How do you feel when you complete a big project?** (Great; good; like I can do anything.)

● **Have you ever found that a project was too big or too hard? What happened?** (Yes, I wanted to build a bookcase for my mom, but I couldn't finish it; yes, I tried to put on a circus in our basement, but it took too much work, and I couldn't train my dog to do anything.)

### Teacher Tip
If, after five to seven minutes, your class still hasn't spread the web to all corners of the room, stop and proceed to the discussion. Be sure to talk about the frustrations of not reaching a goal even after trying hard.

### Teacher Tip
Be sure that children understand that they don't need to work to earn their way to heaven and that we try to please God out of love for him and because we're thankful for what he has done for us.

Say: **All of us have big projects that we work hard on. Sometimes we do our best, and we finish big projects. That makes us feel great. Sometimes, even when we do our best, we can't finish, or we can't do things as well as we'd like. That makes us feel bad. But if we work hard, God will be pleased even if we don't do a perfect job. God wants us to keep on trying and working hard.** ✦ **God is pleased when we do our best.**

# GOD'S STRENGTH 📖

## (up to 12 minutes)

Say: **Listen to this verse about strength.** Read Philippians 4:13 and say: **Let's find out how God will help us do our best.**

Have the children line up on one side of the room along a masking tape line. Give each child a piece of *plastic foam.*

Say: **Do your best to toss the foam across the room.** Have each child stand on the masking tape line and toss a piece of foam. Give children each a *black insect* to mark where the foam pieces land. Have children retrieve the foam pieces and try again, repositioning their *black insects* after the second toss. Let the children try three times to toss the *plastic foam* pieces across the room. Then put all but one of the foam pieces back in the Learning Lab.

Tape the remaining foam piece to the *big eraser.* Have each child toss the eraser and foam piece across the room. (Remove any objects that might be hit in this process. Also, caution the children not to throw the eraser too high, too hard, or at anything.)

As each child tosses the eraser and foam piece, use a new black bug to mark where they land. (After every child has thrown the eraser, you will have two lines of black bugs. One line will show where the foam pieces landed when they were thrown alone. The second line will show where the foam piece landed when it was taped to the *big eraser.)*

Say: **Look how far apart the lines are.** Have the children sit down as you return the eraser, the foam piece, and the black bugs to the Learning Lab. Ask:

● **What made the difference between the first line of bugs and the second line?** (The second line shows what happened when we tossed the eraser; it was easier to throw the eraser.)

● **What did you think when you tossed the foam piece as hard as you could and it landed only a few feet away?** (I was disappointed; I knew that it wouldn't go very far because it's so light.)

● **How is tossing the foam like trying hard to do your best but still not doing very well?** (I get upset when I try and try and still don't do well; I feel bad when I don't do well.)

● **Why did the foam piece go farther when it was taped to the eraser?** (The eraser was heavy; it was bigger.)

Read Philipians 4:13 again. Ask:

**LEARNING LAB**

**KEY VERSE** Connection

"Always remember what you have been taught, and don't let go of it. Keep all that you have learned; it is the most important thing in life" (Proverbs 4:13).

First- and second-graders are being challenged by many new things. They may feel overwhelmed at times by all they are expected to learn and remember. Use this Key Verse to encourage them to keep working to overcome challenges with patience and perseverance.

● **How is the weight of the eraser like God's help and strength?** (God's strength helps us go further; God adds his strength to ours.)

Say: **Find a friend and tell him or her about a time God helped you do something hard or about a situation you're facing now that you need God's help to face.**

Give the children time to share. Then bring the class back together and have volunteers share their experiences with the rest of the class.

Say: **All of us face challenges. You found that out when you shared your experiences with each other. We all have tough things we need to do—things such as doing our chores every day without being reminded, following God when we're tempted to do wrong, and being kind to a person who's always mean to us.**  **God is pleased when we do our best to face those challenges. And God promises to give us all the help we need to do our best.**

**THE POINT**

We believe Christian education extends beyond the classroom into the home. Photocopy the "Growing Together" handout (p. 129) for this week and send it home with your children. Encourage children and parents to use the handout to plan meaningful activities on this week's topic. Follow up the "Growing Together" activities next week by asking children what their families did.

# CLOSING

## ENCOURAGEMENTS 📖

**(up to 10 minutes)**

**LEARNING LAB**

Ask:
● **What did you learn today?** (I learned that God wants me to work hard; God likes me to try my best.)

Say: **Listen to this passage from the Bible. Be ready to say what we can do to help each other do our best.** Read Hebrews 10:24-25. Ask:

● **What can we do to help each other do our best?** (Encourage each other; tell each other to do good; go to church together).

Hold up the *rainbow shark* and say: **Sharks never stop to rest. They have to swim all the time because that's how they breathe. When a shark** swims, water goes inside the shark and the shark takes oxygen from the water. Sharks are persistent; they are always moving, no matter what. Let's use this *rainbow shark* as an award for always doing our best, even when we are tired and want to stop.

Have the children sit in two lines facing each other. Have the first child in line award the shark to the child who is facing him or her and say, "I give you this shark because you do your best to... Keep up the good work." Be ready to whisper suitable encouragements to the child giving the award. Suitable encouragements affirm children's efforts to do good work. For example, Cindy might be working hard to spell well. Andy might be working hard to be kind to other children.

Have the child who received the shark present it to the child who gave it to him or her. Then have the pair pass the shark to the next pair of children.

When the shark has been awarded to each child, say: **You have all done a great job of encouraging each other. Now let's ask God to help us do our best.**

Pray: **God, we want to please you in all we do. We know that ★ you are pleased when we do our best. Help us work hard to do our best every day. And help us encourage one another, too. Amen.**

 **THE POINT** ★

# SCHOOLHOUSE NAME TAGS

Photocopy this page and cut out the name tags as indicated. Have children color their name tags and write their names on them.

## School 10:

**God is pleased when we do our best.**

### Key Verse

*"Always remember what you have been taught, and don't let go of it. Keep all that you have learned; it is the most important thing in life" (Proverbs 4:13).*

# GROWING TOGETHER

Today your child learned that God is pleased when we do our best. The children discovered that doing a good job takes persistence, patience, and hard work. They also learned that it's important to encourage one another. Use these ideas this week to encourage your child to do his or her best.

## MEDALS
• • • • • • • •

Give your child this "medal" when you notice that he or she has worked hard. Write a note of praise and encouragement on a slip of paper. Wrap the paper around a cookie, then wrap the cookie in aluminum foil. Cut an inverted V in the bottom of a 3-inch section of wide ribbon. Tape the ribbon to the cookie so that it looks like a medal. Put the cookie medal in your child's lunch box as a surprise.

## ART FRAMES
• • • • • • • • • •

Make this easy frame to display your child's artwork. Cut a window in one side of a large Manila envelope, leaving a border of 2 inches. Have your child use stickers or stamps and a stamp pad to decorate the border. Have your child choose the artwork to be displayed in the frame, then place the art inside the envelope so that it shows through the opening. Next week, have your child place a new piece of artwork in the frame on top of the first picture. Use the same frame until the envelope is full, then make a new one.

## STAR AWARDS
• • • • • • • • • •

Cut a star shape out of cardboard and cover the star with aluminum foil. Read Philippians 2:15 and talk about how the members of your family can do their best to shine like stars. One at a time, have each family member hold the star while other family members tell how he or she has lived out Philippians 2:15. Do this weekly to encourage each other to please God and to affirm each other's efforts.

## CONGRATULATIONS!
• • • • • • • • • • • • • • • • • • • • • •

Recognize your child's hard work and achievement by painting congratulations on your car windows or on your child's bedroom window. Mix a spoonful of dish-washing liquid into a cup of tempera paint and paint away. The paint will easily wash off the windows.

# C·A·R·E F·O·R

# O·T·H·E·R·S

Aug 10th

## THE POINT
God is pleased
when we care
about others.

It's important to say The Point just as it's written in each
activity. Repeating The Point over and over will help children
remember it and apply it to their lives.

## THE BIBLE BASIS:
2 Kings 5:1-14. A slave girl helps Naaman.

Naaman was the commander of the Aramean army. He was honored and
respected by the king because of his military ability. The Bible says
that he was mighty and brave. But Naaman suffered from a serious
skin disease. A young girl who had been taken captive during an
Aramean raid on Israel served Naaman's wife. The young girl had great
faith in the prophet Elisha. She told her mistress that if Naaman could
meet with the prophet, surely he could cure Naaman of the disease.
Naaman traveled to Samaria to find Elisha. Naaman reluctantly followed
Elisha's instructions and was cured. Because of the young girl's faith in
Elisha and her willingness to speak up, Naaman found the cure he
sought.

The first- and second-graders in your class may think of themselves as
too young to do important things. They're too young to stay by themselves. They're too young to go where they please when they please. But
like the young Israelite girl, these children aren't too young to have a
powerful influence on their world. They can make a difference by caring
for others at home, in their neighborhoods, and at school. They can tell
others about God. They can fight injustice. And they can be persuasive
peacemakers. Use this lesson to help children learn to care for others.

Other Scriptures used in this lesson are John 13:35; 1 Thessalonians
3:12; and James 2:8.

## KEY VERSE
for Lessons 10–13

"Always remember what
you have been taught, and
don't let go of it. Keep all
that you have learned; it is
the most important thing
in life"
(Proverbs 4:13).

# GETTING THE POINT

Children will

- do caring things for one another,
- learn how to love their neighbors as themselves, and  *old towels*
- discover how loving others shows they're God's children.

*Cheerios*
*raisins*
*copy p.139 x1*
*plain sugar cookies*
*(icing)*
*sprinkle candies/colored sugar*
*knives*

Before the lesson, collect the items from the Learning Lab for the activities you plan to use. Refer to the pictures in the margin to see what each item looks like.

## THIS LESSON AT A GLANCE

| SECTION | MINUTES | WHAT CHILDREN WILL DO | LEARNING LAB SUPPLIES | CLASSROOM SUPPLIES |
|---------|---------|----------------------|----------------------|--------------------|
| WELCOME TIME | up to 5 | **Welcome!**—Receive a warm welcome from the teacher and make name tags. | | "Schoolhouse Name Tags" (p. 128), markers, scissors, tape |
| ATTENTION GRABBER | up to 10 | **Caring Actions**—Play a game in which they do caring things for each other and learn that God is pleased when they care about others. | Black insect | "Caring Actions" handout (p. 139), paper, pencils |
| BIBLE EXPLORATION & APPLICATION | up to 12 📖 | **Naaman's Disease**—Listen to the story of Naaman from 2 Kings 5:1-14 and see how a young servant girl cared for her master. | | Bible |
| | up to 10 📖 | **"Who Am I?" Interviews**—Guess people's jobs by listening to what they do, listen to John 13:35, and talk about situations in which they can show they are God's children by their love for others. | Cassette: "Who Am I?" "Caring Situations" | Bible, cassette player |
| | up to 13 📖 | **Others as Ourselves**—Listen to James 2:8, decorate cookies to eat and to give away, and talk about how to love their neighbors as themselves. | | Bibles, cookies, frosting, candies, knives, napkins, markers |
| CLOSING | up to 10 📖 | **Overflowing Love**—Listen to 1 Thessalonians 3:12, say good things about each other as they squeeze water from a foam shape, and talk about how love increases and overflows. | Foam shapes, bubble kit | Bible, basin of water, *old* towels |

Remember to make photocopies of the "Growing Together" handout (p. 140) to send home with your children. "Growing Together" is a valuable tool for helping first- and second-graders talk with their parents about what they're learning in class.

# T·H·E  L·E·S·S·O·N

## WELCOME TIME

### WELCOME!
**(up to 5 minutes)**

- Greet each child individually with an enthusiastic smile.
- Thank each child for coming to class today.
- As children arrive, ask them about last week's "Growing Together" discussion. Use questions such as "How did the members of your family congratulate each other for doing their best?" and "What did you learn about working hard?"
- Say: **Today we're going to learn that** ✦ **God is pleased when we care about others.**
- Help children put their name tags on. If some children weren't in class last week, or if some of the name tags were damaged, photocopy the "Schoolhouse Name Tags" (p. 128) and have children follow the instructions to create new name tags.
- Tell the children that the attention-getting signal you'll use during this lesson is clapping your hands three times. Ask children to respond by clapping their hands three times as they stop talking and focus their attention on you. Rehearse the signal with the children, telling them to respond quickly so you have plenty of time for all the fun activities planned for this lesson.

**THE POINT** ★

## ATTENTION GRABBER

### CARING ACTIONS
**(up to 10 minutes)**

Make one photocopy of the "Caring Actions" handout (p. 139).

Have each child write his or her name on a slip of paper. Make sure the names are legible as you fold the slips and put them inside a container such as the lid of the Learning Lab box.

Have the class sit in a circle. Place the "Caring Actions" handout in the center of the circle. Choose a name from the container. Then stand three feet away from the "Caring Actions" handout and toss a *black insect* onto one of the sec-

**LEARNING LAB**

tions. Read the caring action described in that section and do that action for the person whose name you chose from the container. If the insect doesn't land on a section, toss it again.

Set aside the name you picked from the box. Have the child who received your caring action draw a name from the container and toss an insect onto the handout. Help the child read the appropriate action and perform the caring action for the person whose name he or she drew. Continue until each child's name has been chosen.

If you'd like, play the game again. Then put away the handout, the *black insect,* and the container. Ask:

● **What was it like to do a caring action for someone?** (It was fun; I was embarrassed to do it in front of others; it made me feel good.)

● **When have you done something caring for someone?** (I took flowers to my neighbor; I helped my grandma fold the laundry; I was extra nice to a new girl on the playground.)

● **What was it like to do something caring in real life?** (It was fun; it made me feel good; it helped me make a good friend.)

● **What was it like to receive a caring action?** (That was fun, too; it made me feel like people like me.)

● **When has someone done something caring for you in real life?** (My best friend made me a present when we moved here; my cousins called me on the phone when I was sick.)

Say: **It feels terrific when people do something nice for us. It feels just as good when we do caring things for others. But it's not only nice for us;**  **God is pleased when we care about others. Today we'll learn about a young girl who did something nice for the man she worked for. It was just a little thing, but it changed his entire life. Let's find out what happened.**

 **THE POINT**

 IBLE EXPLORATION & APPLICATION

## NAAMAN'S DISEASE 📖

### (up to 12 minutes)

Open your Bible to 2 Kings 5:1-14. Say: **This is a story about a man named Naaman** (NAY-uh-mun). **Watch carefully during this story and follow my actions.**

**Naaman** (hold your hands in front of you with the backs facing out) **was the commander of the Aramean army. He was honored and respected by his master** (applaud) **because God had helped him be victorious in battle. But Naaman** (display your hands) **had a serious skin disease.**

Naaman's army attacked the Israelites and took a little girl (pat your hand in the air to show how small she was) **captive. The little girl** (pat your hand in the air) **served Naaman's wife** (pretend to slide a ring on your finger).

One day the little girl (pat your hand in the air) **said to her mistress, "I wish that my master, Naaman** (display your hands)**, would go to see the prophet Elisha, a man of God** (point to heaven) **who lives in Samaria. I'm sure that Elisha could heal him."**

**Naaman's wife** (pretend to slide a ring on your finger) **told him about the prophet, and Naaman** (display your hands) **told the king** (pretend to put on a crown) **that he wanted to travel to Samaria to see the prophet. The king gave his permission, and Naaman** (display your hands) **packed gifts of gold, silver, and clothing** (pretend to pack) **to give to the prophet.**

**Naaman** (display your hands) **traveled to Samaria to find the prophet Elisha. When he found Elisha, the prophet said, "Go and wash in the Jordan River** (wiggle your fingers in front of you to show a flowing river) **seven times** (hold up seven fingers)**. Then your skin will be healed—the disease will be gone."**

**Naaman** (display your hands) **was very angry** (make an angry face) **that he had traveled all that way only to be told to take a bath in a dirty river. He had wanted Elisha to pray to God** (fold your hands) **and wave his hand** (wave your hand in the air) **to heal the disease. Naaman** (display your hands) **said, "We have better rivers where I come from. Why can't I wash in them and be clean?"**

**One of Naaman's servants said, "Master, if the prophet had told you to do a great thing, you surely would have done it. Doesn't it make sense to do whatever the prophet tells you to do?"**

**So Naaman** (display your hands) **went to the Jordan River** (wiggle your fingers) **and dipped into it seven times** (dip your hands seven times)**. Then his skin was new and clean again!** (Hold your hands in front of you and show them off, back and front.)

**Because the little servant girl** (pat the air with your hand) **had told about the prophet Elisha, Naaman** (display your hands) **was healed of his disease.**

Ask:

● **What do you think Naaman thought when he saw that he'd been cured?** (I think he was excited; I think he praised God; I bet he was glad he went to meet Elisha.)

● **What do you think he said to the servant girl when he got home?** (I think he said thank you; I think that he freed her; I think he gave her a present and said thank you.)

● **All the servant girl did was tell Naaman's wife about the prophet Elisha; what small acts of kindness can you do?** (I can pray for my friends; I can use my quiet voice when my mom's resting; I can take care of my little brother when Dad's busy.)

Say: **Sometimes little kindnesses can have big results. All the servant girl did was mention Elisha to Naaman's wife, but look what happened. Naaman was cured of a terrible disease.** ✦ **God is pleased when we**

**THE POINT** ★

care about others, even when we do small things to show that we care. Let's find out why God wants us to care about others.

## "WHO AM I?" INTERVIEWS 📖
### (up to 10 minutes)

Cue the *cassette tape* to "Who Am I?" During this segment, the children will listen to three different people describe their jobs. After each person finishes, the children will guess his or her occupation.

Listen to the first speaker, then stop the tape and have the children guess the person's occupation. Do the same thing with the second and third speakers.

When the children have guessed all three occupations, ask:
● **How did you guess what those people do every day?**

Say: **Listen to this verse and tell me how people will know that we're Christians.** Read John 13:35. Ask:
● **How will people know that we're God's children—Christians?** (By our love; by the good things we do for others.)

Say: **Let's listen to the tape again. This time, someone will tell us about three situations in which we can show that we're God's children by the caring things we do. When I turn off the tape, you'll all have a chance to think of a caring action that fits the situation that has just been described.**

During the next tape segment, "Caring Situations," there will be three situations for the children to discuss. Stop the tape after each situation is explained. Form pairs and have the pairs talk about what they could do in that situation to show they are God's children. Have volunteers share their ideas with the rest of the class.

Read John 13:35 again. Then say: **You thought of a lot of great ways to show others we care about them. How we behave shows what's important to us. It shows what we're like inside. When we care about others, it shows that we're God's children. That's why**  **God is pleased when we care about others.**

### Teacher Tip
If you have time, have the pairs think of short skits to show the class their responses.

★ **THE POINT**

## OTHERS AS OURSELVES 📖
### (up to 13 minutes)

Bring plain cookies, tubs of prepared frosting, small candies, knives, and paper napkins to class.

Say: **Listen to this Bible verse.** Read James 2:8. **Let's see how we can love our neighbors as ourselves.**

Give the children each two cookies and have them decorate the cookies with the icing and small candies. While the children are decorating their cookies, ask:

- **What does it mean to love your neighbor as yourself?** (It means to be nice all the time; it means to treat others the way you want to be treated.)
- **Who is your neighbor?** (The person next door; the person sitting next to me at school; everyone.)
- **What caring things can you do for your neighbor?** (I can say, "Good morning"; I can help my next-door neighbor take out his trash; I can give cookies to my friends.)

When the cookies are decorated, tell the children to keep one for themselves. Then have each student write the words of James 2:8 on a napkin and wrap the second cookie in the napkin to give to a friend or neighbor (not a family member).

Say: **After class, give your wrapped cookie to a neighbor or friend.** Ask:
- **How is giving one cookie away like loving your neighbor as yourself?** (I'm giving someone else the same thing I gave myself; I decorated both cookies the same, so we get the same treat; I'm giving away a cookie, and I'd like someone to give me a cookie sometime.)

Say: **When we give the same kind of caring to others that we give to ourselves, then we are loving our neighbors as ourselves. You all will show your neighbors and friends you care for them when you give them your cookies.** ✦ God is pleased when we care about others.

## KEY VERSE
### Connection

"Always remember what you have been taught, and don't let go of it. Keep all that you have learned; it is the most important thing in life" (Proverbs 4:13).

First- and second-graders have a great capacity for caring for others, and they usually jump at any opportunity to help! Use this Key Verse to encourage them to act on what they've learned by always caring for others and finding ways to help.

---

**W**e believe Christian education extends beyond the classroom into the home. **GROWING TOGETHER** Photocopy the "Growing Together" handout (p. 140) for this week and send it home with your children. Encourage children and parents to use the handout to plan meaningful activities on this week's topic. Follow up the "Growing Together" activities next week by asking children what their families did.

---

# **C**LOSING

**LEARNING LAB**

## OVERFLOWING LOVE 📖

### (up to 10 minutes)

Do this activity on the church lawn if it's warm outside. If you do it inside, provide towels.

Gather the children in a circle. Set a basin of water, the six *foam shapes,* and the shallow dish from the *bubble kit* in the middle of the circle. Ask:

● **What did you learn today?** (I learned that I should be nice to others; I learned to do caring things to show that I'm God's child.)

Say: **Listen to this Bible verse and be ready to tell me what God does to our love.** Read 1 Thessalonians 3:12 from the New International Version: **"May the Lord make your love increase and overflow for each other and for everyone else, just as ours does for you."** Ask:

● **What does God do to our love for others?** (He makes it get bigger; he makes it overflow.)

Say: ★ **God is pleased when we care about others. When we do, our love will increase and overflow.**

One by one, have each child come to the center of the circle, plunge a *foam shape* into the water, and squeeze the shape underwater to release air bubbles and help it fill with water. Then have the child hold the *foam shape* over the shallow dish of the *bubble kit* and squeeze or wring the *foam shape* so that water is released. As the water streams out of the *foam shape,* have the child say a caring thing about the next child in the circle. For example, a child might say, "Cathy, I like being friends with you because you tell good jokes." Be ready to help spark children's ideas.

Continue until everyone has been affirmed and the water overflows the shallow dish. Then put away the *foam shapes,* the *bubble kit,* and the basin of water. Read 1 Thessalonians 3:12 again. Ask:

● **What was it like to have someone say nice things to you?** (It was good; I was embarrassed, but I liked what she said.)

● **How did it feel to say nice things to others?** (It felt good; it was nice; it made me feel friendly.)

● **What do you think this means: "May your love increase and overflow"?** (It means that love should get bigger and bigger; it means that we should love more.)

● **How is overflowing water like overflowing love?** (There has to be a lot of both of them for them to overflow; it's fun when they overflow.)

Say: **When we do caring things for each other and when we say nice things to each other, the love that is in our group will grow bigger and bigger. Each of us can take a part in making the love grow. Each of us can please God by caring for each other. Let's pray.**

Pray: **God, thank you for loving us. We would like to please you and show our love for you by caring for each other. Show us how we can care for each other. Amen.**

## THE POINT

### Teacher Tip

Encourage the children to take this activity seriously; don't allow them to throw the water.

# CARING ACTIONS

| | |
|---|---|
| Say, "You're a great person!" | Shake a hand. |
| Smile. | Pat someone on the back. |
| Give a high five. | Say, "God loves you." |
| Say, "I'm glad you're my friend." | Give a quick shoulder rub. |

## SCHOOL 11:

**God is pleased when we care about others.**

### KEY VERSE

*"Always remember what you have been taught, and don't let go of it. Keep all that you have learned; it is the most important thing in life"* (Proverbs 4:13).

## GROWING TOGETHER

## I·N T·O·U·C·H

Today your child learned that it's good to do kind things for others. The children discovered that no matter how small their caring acts are, they will be appreciated by the recipients and by God. Use these ideas in your home this week to encourage caring actions.

### KINDNESS CHORE

If you use a chore chart with your child, consider adding the "chore" of doing a kind deed every day. Making a regular effort to care about others develops a lifelong habit. Have your child choose what to do and who to do it for. You'll be amazed at your child's creativity and thoughtfulness.

### GOODNESS STREAM

Amos 5:24b says, "Let goodness flow like a stream that never stops." On a hot day this week, drape a garden hose over a clothesline, set up a sprinkler in your back yard, or take a trip to a nearby creek or swimming pool. Talk about how a good deed is refreshing to the giver and to the recipient. Mention several good deeds that you and your child can do for someone else. Then enjoy running through the sprinkler, wading in the creek, or jumping in the pool.

### SWEET KINDNESS

Make refreshing lemonade on a hot summer afternoon. Have your child press down on a lemon and roll it back and forth on the kitchen counter. Then cut the lemon in half and squeeze all the juice out. Do the same with two  more lemons and an orange. While you're rolling and squeezing the lemons, taste the lemon juice and talk about how troubles can make people feel. Then stir the lemon and orange juice with a cup of sugar. Taste the juice again and talk about how caring for others can change sourness into sweetness. Stir the juice mixture into two quarts of water and serve it over ice.

### TO ME, TO YOU

Play this game to illustrate John 15:12b: "Love each other as I have loved you." Have your family sit in a circle. Do a loving action, such as a five-second shoulder rub, for the person sitting next to you, then have him or her do the same action for the next person. After the action has come full circle, have the next person choose a different loving action, such as a pat on the back. Continue until everyone has initiated a loving action.

# C·O·M·E A·N·D
# L·E·A·R·N!

*Aug 17th*
*teach*

It's important to say The Point just as it's written in each activity. Repeating The Point over and over will help children remember it and apply it to their lives.

## THE BIBLE BASIS:

Daniel 1:3-20. Daniel and his friends study in the king's court.

After King Nebuchadnezzar of Babylon attacked and conquered Judah, he brought back thousands of Israelites to live in Babylon. He commanded his chief officer to bring into his palace well-educated, young Israelite men from good families. For three years, Nebuchadnezzar had them groomed for positions in his court. At the end of their training, the king found that Daniel and his friends surpassed all the others in their knowledge and understanding.

The children in your class are just beginning their formal education. Their training will last a lot longer than the three years that Daniel and his friends spent in training in the king's palace. With God's help, Daniel and his friends were able to learn a great deal. With God's help, the children in your class will begin to learn the skills that are necessary for them to be successful and responsible citizens. Use this lesson to help children see that God cares about learning. Show the children that in working hard at school, they are preparing themselves for lives of service to their king—the God of the universe.

Other Scriptures used in this lesson are Proverbs 10:14a; Proverbs 24:13-14; 2 Timothy 1:13; and Hebrews 8:10.

## KEY VERSE
### for Lessons 10–13

"Always remember what you have been taught, and don't let go of it. Keep all that you have learned; it is the most important thing in life"
(Proverbs 4:13).

# GETTING THE POINT

Children will

- learn the value of following God's true teaching,

- discover what God wants to write on their hearts, and

- see that they can soak up knowledge like a napkin soaks up paint.

Before the lesson, collect the items from the Learning Lab for the activities you plan to use. Refer to the pictures in the margin to see what each item looks like.

# THIS LESSON AT A GLANCE

| SECTION | MINUTES | WHAT CHILDREN WILL DO | LEARNING LAB SUPPLIES | CLASSROOM SUPPLIES |
|---|---|---|---|---|
| WELCOME TIME | up to 5 | **Welcome!**—Receive a warm welcome from the teacher and make name tags. | | "Schoolhouse Name Tags" (p. 128), markers, scissors, tape |
| ATTENTION GRABBER | up to 10 | **Patterns**—Listen to 2 Timothy 1:13, play a rhythm game, and talk about the pattern of true teaching. | Castanets | Bible |
| BIBLE EXPLORATION & APPLICATION | up to 13 | **Daniel and His Friends Learn**—Hear the story of Daniel 1:3-20 and talk about why it's important to learn and what they can do to be better learners. | Cassette: "Daniel and His Friends Learn" | Bible, cassette player |
| | up to 10 | **Heart Writings**—Make symbols of learning on heart pictures, listen to Hebrews 8:10, and talk about what God would like to write on their inner hearts. | *Make heart from pattern on p. 145 and copy for each child* | Bible, paper, pencil, tape, crayons or markers |
| | up to 12 | **Soak It Up**—Make pictures showing how they can "soak up" knowledge, listen to Proverbs 10:14a, then talk about how they can soak up the things that God wants to teach them. | Paint set | Bible, paper napkins |
| CLOSING | up to 10 | **Future Hopes**—Listen to Proverbs 24:13-14, think about their plans for the future, and be affirmed for the special futures God has planned for them. | Honey straw, cassette: "Help Me Walk in Your Way," "Lyrics Poster" | Bible, scissors, cassette player |

Remember to make photocopies of the "Growing Together" handout (p. 148) to send home with your children. "Growing Together" is a valuable tool for helping first- and second-graders talk with their parents about what they're learning in class.

# T·H·E  L·E·S·S·O·N

ELCOME TIME

## WELCOME!
### (up to 5 minutes)

- Greet each child individually with an enthusiastic smile.
- Thank each child for coming to class today.
- As children arrive, ask them about last week's "Growing Together" discussion. Use questions such as "What did you learn about caring for others?" and "How did you care for your family last week?"
- Say: **Today we're going to learn that ✦ learning is important to God.**
- Help children put on their name tags. If some children weren't in class last week, or if some of the name tags were damaged, photocopy the "Schoolhouse Name Tags" (p. 128) and have children follow the instructions to create new name tags.
- Tell the children that the attention-getting signal you'll use during this lesson is clapping your hands three times. Ask children to respond by clapping their hands three times as they stop talking and focus their attention on you. Rehearse the signal with the children, telling them to respond quickly so you have plenty of time for all the fun activities planned for this lesson.

**THE POINT ✦**

**A**TTENTION GRABBER

## PATTERNS 📖
### (up to 10 minutes)

**LEARNING LAB**

Have the children sit in a circle. Say: **Listen to this verse from the Bible. Be ready to tell me what we can follow.** Read 2 Timothy 1:13. Ask:
- **What can we follow?** (True teaching; a pattern.)

Say: **Let's have fun following patterns. Listen to the rhythm—the pattern—that I click with the *castanets*. Then, when I say "go," clap the same rhythm with your hands.**

Click a simple rhythm with the *castanets,* such as three slow clicks and two

## BIBLE INSIGHT

Throughout their time in Nebuchadnezzar's court, Daniel and his friends remained faithful to Jewish laws, particularly those concerning idolatry and the consumption of meat that had been offered to idols. Because of their faithfulness, God gave the young men tremendous learning abilities, and he also gave Daniel the ability to receive visions and interpret dreams.

★ **THE POINT**

fast clicks, then have the children clap it. Then click a longer and more complicated rhythm and have the children repeat it. Put the *castanets* away.

Form pairs and have the partners take turns clapping rhythms for each other to follow. Have the pairs play for two or three minutes, then gather the class. Ask:

● **Was it easy or hard to follow the rhythms? Why?** (It was easier as I got used to playing the game; it was hard when the pattern was long.)

● **When the rhythms were hard to follow, what did you do to help yourself repeat it correctly?** (I paid attention; I repeated it slowly; I told my partner to clap it for me again.)

Read 2 Timothy 1:13 again. Ask:

● **What is true teaching?** (God's rules; the Bible; God's will.)

● **How do we follow the pattern of true teaching?** (We obey God; we do what our parents tell us to do; we do right; we do good and kind things for others.)

● **How is following the rhythm in the game we played like following the pattern of true teaching?** (You have to pay attention; you have to listen; you have to do it exactly.)

Say: **Today we're going to talk about learning. We have lots to learn—at school, at church, at home, and from the Bible. When we learn, we do just what we did in this game. We see an example, and we follow it. The story today is about four students who set a good example for those around them and for us. By their example, we'll see that ★ learning is important to God.**

# BIBLE EXPLORATION & APPLICATION

★ **THE POINT**

## DANIEL AND HIS FRIENDS LEARN 📖

### (up to 13 minutes)

Cue the *cassette tape* to "Daniel and His Friends Learn." This segment features the voice of "Daniel," who tells about going to King Nebuchadnezzar's palace to learn with Shadrach, Meshach, and Abednego.

Open your Bible to Daniel 1:3-20 and show the passage to the children. Say: **Listen closely to this story about four young men. Because ★ learning is important to God, point to your brain every time you hear the word "learn" or "learned."**

Play the segment. When the story is over, turn the cassette player off and ask:

● **What did Daniel and his friends do that helped them learn?** (They got help from God; they ate healthy food; they paid attention; they worked hard.)

● **Why was it important for them to learn?** (So they could be good servants in the palace; so they could please God; so they could get good jobs.)

● **Why is it important for you to learn?** (So I know how to do important things when I grow up; so I can get a good job; so I can know about the world; so I can please God.)

● **What can you do to help yourself learn?** (I can eat healthy food just as Daniel did; I can pay attention in school; I can do my homework; I can do my best; I can ask my dad to help me.)

Say: **Everyone goes to school to learn important things such as math, reading, and social studies. When we learn, we're preparing ourselves to do important things, just as Daniel and his friends were preparing to be servants in the king's palace.** ✸ **Learning is important to God. Let's find out what God wants us to learn.**

## HEART WRITINGS 📖

### (up to 10 minutes)

Draw a heart on a sheet of paper, using the heart pattern on this page as a guide. Photocopy the heart you've drawn, making one photocopy for each child.

Tape a heart to each child's back and give each child a crayon or a marker that won't bleed through the paper onto the children's clothing.

Say: **Think of something you've learned about or something you'd like to learn about. Then think of a quick way to draw it. For example, if you've learned how to add, you might draw a plus sign. If you've learned how to read, you could write "ABC" or "read." You'll have five minutes to draw your quick picture on everyone's heart.**

Give children a minute to think of what they'll draw. Be ready to help them think of ideas. Then on "go," have the children quickly draw their pictures on the other children's hearts.

After five minutes, call time by clapping your hands three times. Wait for the children to clap three times and focus their attention on you. Then gather all of the markers or crayons and have the children take the hearts off their backs. Sit in a circle and talk about what each drawing means. Ask:

● **What other things have we learned that we could put on our hearts?** (How to play baseball; how to use a VCR; how to make pancakes.)

Say: ✸**Learning is important to God. Listen to what the Bible says about how God will teach us.**

Read Hebrews 8:10. Ask:

● **What does it mean that God will write teachings on our hearts?** (It means God will teach them to us; it means God thinks it's important to make sure we know them.)

● **How was writing on each other's hearts the same or different from how God writes on our hearts?** (We just wrote on paper, but God writes things on our insides; God has lots to teach us, just like there are lots of things written on my paper heart.)

**THE POINT** ✸

## KEY VERSE
### Connection

"Always remember what you have been taught, and don't let go of it. Keep all that you have learned; it is the most important thing in life" (Proverbs 4:13).

First- and second-graders are beginning to face more new challenges in school. They're beginning to discover that they will use the concepts they are learning now for the rest of their lives. Use this Key Verse to remind kids of the importance of taking in all the information and wisdom that's being offered to them.

**THE POINT** ✸

● **What kinds of teachings do you think God would like to put on our hearts?** (Things about Jesus; how to do good; how to please him; how to worship him; things about himself.)

● **What can we do with the teachings that God writes on our hearts?** (We can tell others about them; we can do the good things that God teaches us about.)

Redistribute the markers or crayons. Have each child quickly draw symbols of or write words about the teachings that God will write on their hearts. For example, children might draw a cross, a manger, Jesus, or an angel; they might write "care," "love," "kind," "learn," or "share."

Say: **There are so many things for us to learn. It was fun to write what we've learned on each other's hearts. It will be just as fun to learn the things that God wants to write on our inner hearts.** ✦ **Learning is important to God. He has much to teach us. Let's find out how we can learn more and more.**

 **THE POINT**

## SOAK IT UP 📖

### (up to 12 minutes)

**LEARNING LAB**

Put a little water in each of the paints in the *paint set*. Use the end of the *paintbrush* to stir the water to dissolve the pigment. Keep adding water to the paints throughout this activity.

Give each child a paper napkin. Show the children how to fold a napkin two or three times. Then dip each corner in paint and watch as the napkin soaks it up. After the children have folded and dipped their napkins, have them unfold them and look at the pretty designs the paints have made.

Put the *paint set* away and set the napkins aside to dry.

Say: **These plain napkins have become beautiful works of art because they soaked up the paint. Listen to this Bible verse.** Read Proverbs 10:14a from the New International Version: **"Wise men store up knowledge."** Ask:

● **How are we like the paper napkins—how can we store up or soak up knowledge like the napkins soaked up the paint?** (We can work hard to learn new things every day; we can study at school; we can pay attention.)

● **What kinds of knowledge should we soak up?** (How to read; how to do math; how to please God.)

● **What do you think we'll be like when we soak up knowledge?** (We'll be smart; we'll be ready for anything; we'll be perfect; we'll get A's on all of our tests.)

● **What can you use your knowledge for?** (To help others; to do exciting things when I grow up; to get good grades in school; to please my parents.)

● **Why does God want us to soak up knowledge?** (So we'll be ready to serve him; so we'll be ready to do good things; so we'll know how to please him.)

Say: **Every day, we can pretend we're like little napkins, soaking up all of the knowledge we can find.** ✦ **Learning is important to God. Let's ask God to help us learn.**

> ### Teacher Tip
> If you've run out of paints, mix food coloring with water in small bowls until the water is brightly colored. Caution the children to be careful not to get the paint on their clothes.

 **THE POINT**

We believe Christian education extends beyond the classroom into the home. **GROWING TOGETHER** Photocopy the "Growing Together" handout (p. 148) for this week and send it home with your children. Encourage children and parents to use the handout to plan meaningful activities on this week's topic. Follow up the "Growing Together" activities next week by asking children what their families did.

# CLOSING

## FUTURE HOPES 📖

### (up to 10 minutes)

Ask:
● **What did you learn today?** (I learned that learning is important; I learned that learning can be fun; I learned that God wants me to soak up knowledge.)

Gather the children in a circle and sit down. Say: **Listen to what the Bible says about wisdom and knowledge.**

Read Proverbs 24:13-14. Then say: **Take a moment to think about how you can use knowledge and wisdom in your life.**

Sit quietly for a minute, then say: **Turn to a friend and tell him or her what you would like to do in the future.** Read Proverbs 24:13-14 again. Then snip the end of the *honey straw* and put a drop or two of honey on each child's finger. Have each child eat the honey. Then ask:

● **Why do you think the Bible says that wisdom is sweet?** (Because it's good for you; it's sweet so you'll want more of it.)

● **How will knowledge, wisdom, and learning help bring about a good future?** (They'll make me smart; they'll make me ready for anything.)

Affirm each child. If there's more honey in the *honey straw,* put another drop of it on each child's finger as you say: (Child's name), **God has planned great things for your future, and God made you for a special purpose. Store up sweet wisdom to help you achieve great things for God.**

After every child has been affirmed, use the *cassette tape* to lead the class in singing "Help Me Walk in Your Way" as a closing prayer. Hang the "Lyrics Poster" on the wall and point to the words as you sing them. Have the children say "amen" together at the end of the song.

**LEARNING LAB**

**SCHOOL 12:**

Learning is important to God.

## KEY VERSE

*"Always remember what you have been taught, and don't let go of it. Keep all that you have learned; it is the most important thing in life" (Proverbs 4:13).*

# GROWING TOGETHER

Permission to photocopy this handout from Group's Hands-On Bible Curriculum™ for Grades 1 and 2 granted for local church use. Copyright © Group Publishing, Inc., P.O. Box 481, Loveland, CO 80539.

## I·N T·O·U·C·H

Today your child learned that knowledge, wisdom, and learning are important to God. The children learned that they can soak up knowledge to prepare for the future God has planned for them. They also discovered that God has important things that he wants to teach them by writing those things on their hearts. Use these ideas to help your child value learning.

### STUDY SPACE
• • • • • • • •

Create a private study space on a table. Cut the top and one side from a sturdy box with tall sides. Discard the pieces you've cut from the box. Paint the box and decorate it. Cut cereal boxes in half and staple them to the inside of the box to hold crayons, markers, and pencils. Glue a Manila envelope to the inside of the box to hold paper. To make a more stable writing area, have a piece of particleboard cut to fit into the bottom of the box.

### EVERYDAY LEARNING
• • • • • • • • • •

At dinner every night this week, have family members each mention one thing they learned that day. Even if this sends your child on a mad dash to the encyclopedia just before dinner, he or she will see that learning can be fun and can occur every day. As you offer thanks for the meal, also offer thanks that God has given your family minds that can learn and grow.

### HEALTHY BODIES AND MINDS
• • • • • • • • • • • • • • • • • • •

People learn best when their bodies are healthy and rested. Help your child learn by making sure that he or she gets plenty of sleep—at least 10 hours. One morning, treat your child to this fun and healthy breakfast. Mash half of a banana with a big spoonful of peanut butter. Toast two toaster waffles, then spread them with the banana mixture. Put the waffles together to make a sandwich, cut the  sandwich in half, and serve it with a glass of fruit juice.

### ENDLESS QUESTIONS
• • • • • • • • • •

Have your family members each write down at least one question they want to know the answer to. For example, someone might write, "Why are clouds white?" See how many of the questions your family can answer this week. Start a notebook in which family members can write bits of interesting information they come across, such as how much an ostrich egg weighs or how much rain your town gets in a year. Have fun quizzing each other.

# T·E·L·L T·H·E
# T·R·U·T·H

Aug 24th

## THE POINT
God is pleased when we tell the truth.

It's important to say The Point just as it's written in each activity. Repeating The Point over and over will help children remember it and apply it to their lives.

## THE BIBLE BASIS: 📖
Daniel 3:1-30. Shadrach, Meshach, and Abednego refuse to worship false gods.

It was hard to worship God in Babylon. Many false gods were honored, and it took dedication to remain true to God. It was even harder when King Nebuchadnezzar issued an ultimatum to worship his statue or be killed. But Shadrach, Meshach, and Abednego refused to worship the statue and faced the consequences—a torturous death in a fiery furnace. The three men were saved by their decision to live according to the truth; God protected them from the flames. Nebuchadnezzar was amazed by the divine protection that these three humble men experienced, and he decreed that no one in his kingdom would ever again speak against the God of Shadrach, Meshach, and Abednego.

Children are pressured to abandon the truth about God, too. It's not easy to stand up for God at school, at play, and sometimes even at home. But being truthful means doing what's right and standing up for God's truth. Being truthful also means to honestly live out what we believe every day. Have fun helping the kids in your class learn to tell the truth with their words and with their actions.

Other Scriptures used in this lesson are Psalm 25:5; Proverbs 12:19; 2 Timothy 4:3-4; and 3 John 3-4.

## KEY VERSE
for Lessons 10–13

"Always remember what you have been taught, and don't let go of it. Keep all that you have learned; it is the most important thing in life"
(Proverbs 4:13).

# GETTING THE POINT

Children will

● see that all lies will eventually be discovered,

● learn that truth will continue forever, and

● learn about following the way of truth.

Before the lesson, collect the items from the Learning Lab for the activities you plan to use. Refer to the pictures in the margin to see what each item looks like.

# THIS LESSON AT A GLANCE

| SECTION | MINUTES | WHAT CHILDREN WILL DO | LEARNING LAB SUPPLIES | CLASSROOM SUPPLIES |
|---------|---------|------------------------|------------------------|---------------------|
| WELCOME TIME | up to 5 | **Welcome!**—Receive a warm welcome from the teacher and make name tags. | | "Schoolhouse Name Tags" (p. 128), markers, scissors, tape |
| ATTENTION GRABBER | up to 10 | **Whoppers**—Tell whoppers to each other and create bubbles to learn that lies will always burst. | Bubble kit | Dish soap, water |
| BIBLE EXPLORATION & APPLICATION | up to 13 | **The Fiery Furnace**—Act out the story of Shadrach, Meshach, and Abednego from Daniel 3:1-30 and see how they lived the truth. | Jump-rope, lariat | Bible, tape, construction paper, scissors |
| | up to 10 | **Nebuchadnezzar Says**—Play a version of Simon Says to practice listening for the truth and listen to 3 John 3-4. | Cassette: "Nebu-chadnezzar Says" | Bible, cassette player |
| | up to 12 | **Tested Truth**—Talk about truths and lies they've told, then hear Proverbs 12:19 and find out that truth lasts forever. | Big eraser | Bible, paper, pens, pencils, newsprint, tape |
| CLOSING | up to 10 | **Guide and Teach**—See that by themselves, they can get confused about the truth, then learn from Psalm 25:5 that God will guide them and teach them to tell the truth. | Lariat | Bible |

Remember to make photocopies of the "Growing Together" handout (p. 159) to send home with your children. "Growing Together" is a valuable tool for helping first- and second-graders talk with their parents about what they're learning in class.

# T·H·E  L·E·S·S·O·N

## WELCOME TIME

### WELCOME!

**(up to 5 minutes)**

- Greet each child individually with an enthusiastic smile.
- Thank each child for coming to class today.
- As children arrive, ask them about last week's "Growing Together" discussion. Use questions such as "What did your family learn last week?" and "What did you discover about learning?"
- Say: **Today we're going to learn that**  **God is pleased when we tell the truth.**
- Help children put on their name tags. If some children weren't in class last week, or if some of the name tags were damaged, photocopy the "Schoolhouse Name Tags" (p. 128) and have children follow the instructions to create new name tags.
- Tell the children that the attention-getting signal you'll use during this lesson is clapping your hands three times. Ask children to respond by clapping their hands three times as they stop talking and focus their attention on you. Rehearse the signal with the children, telling them to respond quickly so you have plenty of time for all the fun activities planned for this lesson.

**THE POINT**

## ATTENTION GRABBER

### WHOPPERS

**(up to 10 minutes)**

Mix two parts dish soap with one part water. Put the mixture in the shallow dish of the *bubble kit*.

Gather the children in a circle around the *bubble kit*. Say: **Today we're talking about truth and lies. Sometimes we call lies "whoppers," especially if they're big lies that are really hard to believe. Let's think of some whoppers that people might tell. I'll start us off with one. Someone might say that he flew to the moon on his special motorized bicycle.**

After you suggest a whopper that someone might tell, dip the large bubble

**LEARNING LAB**

wand in the bubble mixture and wave it slowly in the air to create one huge bubble. Wait until the bubble pops. Then give each child a chance to suggest a "whopper." After each child's turn, have him or her make a huge bubble. Wait until it pops before going on to the next child.

After every child has had a turn, put away the *bubble kit.* Ask:

● **What do you think when you hear someone tell a whopper?** (I know it isn't true; I don't believe it even at the beginning.)

● **Even though the soap bubbles were big and pretty, they popped quickly. How are lies like soap bubbles?** (You know that they won't last; someone always knows the truth, and the lie falls apart; they don't have any truth in them, so they break.)

● **Have you ever told a lie that was found out? Tell us about it.** (I told my mom that I was playing after school, but she found out that I was in detention instead; I told all my friends that Michael Jordan is my cousin, but they found out he isn't.)

● **Why do people tell lies?** (To keep from getting in trouble; so that people will think they're important; because it's fun.)

● **Why is it wrong to tell lies?** (Because lies cover up the bad things we do; because God doesn't like lies.) *lies hurt people*

Say: **It was fun and exciting to make huge soap bubbles. They were shiny and big and pretty as they floated in the air. Lies can be exciting and fun, too. But just like the soap bubbles, lies are empty—we know they will burst eventually. The truth will always come out. God doesn't want us to tell lies.**  **God is pleased when we tell the truth. Today our story is about three men who told the truth—and lived it. Let's find out what happened.**

 **THE POINT**

# B IBLE EXPLORATION & APPLICATION

**LEARNING LAB**

## THE FIERY FURNACE

### (up to 13 minutes)

Tie the *jump-rope* to the streamer of the *lariat* and wrap them around three chairs to form a triangular area that will represent the fiery furnace. If you have time, make "fire" by fringing sheets of yellow, orange, and red construction paper to hang from the chairs, the *jump-rope,* and the streamer.

Choose three children to be Shadrach, Meshach, and Abednego. Choose one child to be Nebuchadnezzar and another child to be an angel. The rest of the children can be Babylonian leaders.

Open your Bible to Daniel 3:1-30 and show the passage to the children.

Say: **Listen to this story about three men who told the truth. Help me** tell the story by acting it out.

Nebuchadnezzar built a statue that was 90 feet tall. (Have the child playing Nebuchadnezzar pretend to build a tall statue.)

Then he called all of the important people of the country—the leaders, governors, advisors, judges, and rulers—together in front of the statue. (Have the children playing the Babylonian leaders, Shadrach, Meshach, and Abednego gather in front of the "statue.")

Nebuchadnezzar said, "Listen to my command. Whenever you hear music made by horns, flutes, harps, pipes, or other instruments, you must bow down and worship the gold statue that I've made. Anyone who refuses to bow down to the statue will be thrown into the fiery furnace and burned to a crisp." (Have Nebuchadnezzar point at the triangle representing the fiery furnace.)

When the people heard the music, they all bowed down—except for Shadrach, Meshach, and Abednego. (Have the Babylonian leaders kneel and bow down. Have Shadrach, Meshach, and Abednego remain standing.)

The Babylonian leaders told the king that Shadrach, Meshach, and Abednego refused to bow down. They said, "These men won't serve your gods, and they won't worship the gold statue."

Nebuchadnezzar was very angry. (Have Nebuchadnezzar look angry.) He ordered that the three men be brought to him.

Shadrach, Meshach, and Abednego stood before the king. (Have Shadrach, Meshach, and Abednego stand by Nebuchadnezzar.)

(Have Nebuchadnezzar pretend to talk to the three men.) The king said, "Is it true that none of you bowed down to the statue when the music was played? I'll give you another chance. I'll play the music again, and this time, you'd better bow down. If you don't, I'll throw you in the blazing furnace. What god will be able to save you from my power then?"

But Shadrach, Meshach, and Abednego said to the king, "We don't need to defend ourselves to you. If you throw us into the furnace, the God we serve is able to save us. No matter what, we will never bow down to this false god you've made."

This made Nebuchadnezzar even more furious, and he changed his mind about giving the three men another chance. He ordered that the furnace be made seven times hotter than usual. (Have Nebuchadnezzar hold up seven fingers.)

Then he had Shadrach, Meshach, and Abednego thrown into the furnace. (Have Shadrach, Meshach, and Abednego stand in the "furnace." Have the child playing the angel join them.)

Then Nebuchadnezzar jumped to his feet in surprise. He said, "Didn't we tie up three men and throw them in the furnace? I see four men in there!" (Have Nebuchadnezzar jump up in surprise.)

Nebuchadnezzar said, "Look! There are four men in there. None of them is burned. And one of them looks like a son of the gods." (Have Nebuchadnezzar hold up four fingers). Nebuchadnezzar called for the men

# BIBLE INSIGHT

While the book of Daniel is considered to be historically accurate, biblical scholars also consider it to be an apocalyptic work, meaning that it symbolically predicts what will happen in the future. The figure of King Nebuchadnezzar, according to scholars, represents the magnificent head of a great world power who was given many opportunities to recognize the kingdom of God but failed to do so. The book of Daniel foretold the end of man-made kingdoms and the coming of the kingdom of God upon the earth.

to come out of the furnace.

Shadrach, Meshach, and Abednego came out of the furnace. The fire hadn't hurt them at all. Their hair wasn't burned. Their clothes weren't burned, and they didn't even smell like smoke. (Have the three men leave the furnace and stand by Nebuchadnezzar.)

(Have Nebuchadnezzar pretend to talk.) Then Nebuchadnezzar said, "Praise the God of Shadrach, Meshach, and Abednego. Their God sent his angel and saved these men from the fire. These men trusted their God and refused to obey me—even though I'm a king. They were willing to die rather than worship any god other than their own. From now on, no one will speak against the God of Shadrach, Meshach, and Abednego.

Have the children give themselves a round of applause and sit down. Untie the *jump-rope* and *lariat* and put them away. Ask:

● **How did the three men tell the truth?** (They wouldn't bow to the idol; they followed God.)

● **What do you think they thought when the king ordered them to be thrown in the furnace?** (I think they were scared; I think they knew that God would save them.)

● **The three men knew that they might be killed if they told the truth. When is it hard for you to tell the truth?** (When everyone else is lying about something, it's hard to tell the truth; when I know something bad will happen to me if I tell the truth.)

● **What do you think the three men thought when they saw the angel?** (I think they were relieved; I bet they were glad.)

● **God helped these men when they told the truth. How do you think God will help you tell the truth?** (God will make things work out all right; God will give me the courage to tell the truth.)

Say: **Telling the truth isn't always easy. Shadrach, Meshach, and Abednego were willing to face a fiery furnace when they spoke up for the true God and wouldn't bow down to a false god. But God saved them. God will be with us when we tell the truth, too.** ✮ **God is pleased when we tell the truth.**

 **THE POINT**

# NEBUCHADNEZZAR SAYS 📖

## (up to 10 minutes)

**LEARNING LAB**

Cue the *cassette tape* to "Nebuchadnezzar Says." This taped segment will lead the children in a game similar to Simon Says. Have the children stand with plenty of space between them.

Say: **Second Timothy 4:3-4 says that a time will come when people will stop listening to the truth and will start to follow false stories. Let's practice listening for the truth so that we will follow the truth instead of false stories. This game is played a little bit like Simon Says. When you** hear bells, do the action on the tape. When you hear a funny horn sound and the words "Nebuchadnezzar says," don't do the action. Since we want to practice as much as possible, you won't be out if you do the wrong action by mistake. All of us will play the entire game.

Start the tape. After the segment is over, turn off the tape, have the children sit down, and ask:

● **Was it easy or hard to always do the right thing in this game?** (Sometimes I did the wrong thing before I knew it was wrong; I just followed everyone else, so it was easy; I listened carefully, so it was easy; it got harder as the game went faster.)

Say: **In this game, doing what Nebuchadnezzar said was like following a false story.** Ask:

● **What is a false story?** (A lie; something about God that's not true; something that makes us disobey God.)

● **When are you tempted to follow lies or false stories instead of the truth?** (When my friends tell lies, sometimes I go along with them; sometimes adults and important people tell lies, and I believe them.)

● **What is the truth?** (God's Word; anything that's not a lie; good things about God.)

● **How do you follow the truth?** (I'm nice to people; I go to church to learn about God; I try to pray and obey God every day.)

Say: **When the Bible talks about following a false story, it means that some people tell lies about God and persuade others to believe things about God that aren't true. They persuade people to do wrong by telling them that God will be pleased if they do it.**

● **What's a false story that some people might try to get us to follow?** (They might say that God isn't real; they might say that it doesn't really matter if we obey God.)

● **What can we do when others try to get us to follow false stories instead of telling the truth?** (We can get away from them; we can just tell the truth; we can stay with people who help us follow God.)

Say: **We know that ✹ God is pleased when we tell the truth. Part of telling the truth is living for the truth—following God in everything we do. Listen to this verse from the Bible about following the truth.** Read 3 John 3-4.

Say: **I'm glad, too, to see how each of you is following the truth in your life.**

Affirm each child for following God's truth. For example, you might say, "Margie, you give God and me great joy when you follow the way of truth by being polite during class discussions" or "Bill, you give God and me great joy when you follow the way of truth by learning from God's Word."

After each child has been affirmed, say: **It takes practice to be able to follow the truth. Shadrach, Meshach, and Abednego followed the truth when they wouldn't bow down to a false idol. Each of you follows the truth when you obey God. ✹ God is pleased when we tell the truth and live for the truth.**

# KEY VERSE Connection

"Always remember what you have been taught, and don't let go of it. Keep all that you have learned; it is the most important thing in life" (Proverbs 4:13).

First- and second-graders aren't too young to have their beliefs about God challenged. Use this Key Verse to encourage kids to stand up for what they've learned about God and to continue to live out God's Word every day.

THE POINT ✹

THE POINT ✹

# TESTED TRUTH 📖

## (up to 12 minutes)

On a sheet of newsprint, write the word "truth" with a pen and the word "lie" with a pencil. Tape the newsprint on a wall where the children can see it.

Say: **Everyone lies sometimes, and everyone tells the truth sometimes. Think of three times that you lied and three times you told the truth when you could have lied. I'll give you each paper, a pen, and a pencil. Write T three times in pen to stand for the three times you told the truth. Write L three times in pencil to stand for the three times you lied. The newsprint will help you remember what to write in pencil and what to write in pen.**

Give each child paper, a pen, and a pencil. Encourage children to think about three times they told the truth and three times they lied. When everyone has written a T in pen three times and an L in pencil three times, form pairs. Have the children tell their partners about the times they lied and the times they told the truth.

Give the pairs three or four minutes to talk. Then get their attention by clapping three times. Wait for the children to respond and focus their attention on you. Have the children sit in a circle, then ask:

● **What happened when you told the truth?** (I got in trouble; my mom said she was proud that I had told the truth.)

● **What happened when you lied?** (I got away with breaking a glass; I got in trouble because my dad found out I had lied.)

Say: **Sometimes we think we get away with things when we lie—and sometimes we do avoid being punished. But most of the time, our lies are found out and we get in even bigger trouble than we were in before. Even when our parents, teachers, and friends don't know we're lying, God knows. God is disappointed when we tell lies. Telling the truth is important to God. Listen to this Bible verse about truth and lies and be ready to tell me why the truth is better than lies.**

Read Proverbs 12:19 from the New Century Version: "Truth will continue forever, but lies are only for a moment." Ask:

● **Why is the truth better than lies?** (Because it lasts forever; because it's right.)

● **What does the Bible mean when it says that truth will continue forever?** (It means that something that's true will always be true; lies will be found to be wrong, but true things are always true.)

● **What does the Bible mean when it says that lies are only for a minute?** (Lies will be found out; lies don't have any truth in them.)

Say: **Let's show that truth lasts forever but lies are only for a minute.** Have the children pass around the *big eraser.* As it comes to each child, have him or her erase one L from his or her paper and try to erase one T. Continue passing the eraser around the circle until all of the L's have been erased. Put the *big eraser* away.

Say: **Look at your papers—only the T's remain. All of the lies have been erased.** Ask:

● **What truths will last forever?** (God will always be with us; God loves us; any truth that I tell will last forever.)

Say: **There are lots of truths that will last forever. For example, God's Word is truth. No matter what, God's Word will always exist, and it tells us we can count on God's love to last forever.**  **God is pleased when we tell the truth. And we know that the truth lasts forever. We can be proud of ourselves when we tell the truth, especially when it's hard to do.**

**W**e believe Christian education extends beyond the classroom into the home. Photocopy the "Growing Together" handout (p. 159) for this week and send it home with your children. Encourage children and parents to use the handout to plan meaningful activities on this week's topic. Follow up the "Growing Together" activities next week by asking children what their families did.

# CLOSING

## GUIDE AND TEACH 📖

### (up to 10 minutes)

Ask:

● **What did you learn today?** (I learned that what I do can be true; I learned to be true to God; I learned to always tell the truth.)

Have the children stand in a big circle with lots of room between them.

Say: **We know that**  **God is pleased when we tell the truth. But sometimes it's hard to tell the truth. Sometimes it's easier to tell a lie, and sometimes it seems best to tell a lie. But telling lies is never the right thing to do. Think about when it's hard to tell the truth. When we struggle to tell the truth, we feel confused. Watch the** *lariat's* **winding and confused path while you're thinking about how hard it is to tell the truth.**

Hold the *lariat* by the string and swing it in front of you in a random pattern. Make the streamer do circles and dips and squiggles in the air. (You'll have more control over the *lariat* if you hold the string at its midpoint.)

Stop twirling the *lariat* and ask:

● **When is it hard to tell the truth?** (Whenever I'm about to get in trouble; when people are teasing me for going to church; when my friends want me to do something wrong.)

● **How do you feel when you're struggling to tell the truth?** (Confused; frustrated.)

Give each child a chance to move the *lariat* in front of him or her in a random pattern.

Say: **We can feel confused and all mixed up when we're struggling to tell the truth. Our lives can feel like a roller coaster. But God promises to help. Listen to this verse from the Bible.** Read Psalm 25:5.

Say: **God promises to guide us and teach us what is true. Then, instead of being out of control as the *lariat* was before, we'll be on course.** Hold the *lariat* string at its midpoint and twirl the *lariat* in a small circle close to the ground.

Say: **And we'll be able to stand up and tell the truth.** Raise your hand to about waist high as you continue to twirl the *lariat* in a small, horizontal circle. The streamer will rise in the air and look as if it's standing in a tall column.

Give each child a chance to twirl the *lariat* in a small circle near the ground and raise his or her hand so that the streamer rises in the air and looks like it's standing in a tall column. Have the children hold their arms away from their bodies so that the plastic part of the *lariat* doesn't hit them.

Say: **Let's ask God to guide us and teach us to tell the truth, just as Shadrach, Meshach, and Abednego did. To show that we want to tell the truth, let's stand in the shape of a T during this prayer.**

Have the children stand and extend their arms to form T's.

Pray: **God, sometimes it's hard to tell the truth. We feel confused and off course when we struggle to find the truth. But God, we know that you are truth. And we thank you for your promise to guide us in the truth and to keep us on the right path. Help us to stand up for the truth every day. We know that ★ you are pleased when we tell the truth. Amen.**

 **THE POINT**

## SCHOOL 13:

**God is pleased when we tell the truth.**

## KEY VERSE

*"Always remember what you have been taught, and don't let go of it. Keep all that you have learned; it is the most important thing in life" (Proverbs 4:13).*

# GROWING TOGETHER

## I·N T·O·U·C·H

Today your child learned that it's important to tell the truth and to live the truth. The children found out that lies will pass away, but God's truth is enduring. The children also discovered that God will guide them and teach them what is true. Use these ideas in your home this week to help your child learn to tell and live for the truth every day.

## SCHOOL TRUTH

Cut a schoolhouse shape out of construction paper. Use the illustration below as a guide. Talk about how your child can be honest at school. For example, doing one's own work is honest; cheating isn't. Write the ideas on the schoolhouse and hang it up in your child's room.

## COVER-UPS

Put a dot in the center of a piece of paper. Think of a lie that the dot could represent, such as "I didn't eat the last cookie." Then think of another lie that must be told to cover up the first lie, such as "The dog must have eaten it." Cover the dot with a small piece of paper. Continue thinking of bigger and bigger lies. You might end up saying, "A circus parade came down the street, and 11 elephants broke into the house and stole the last cookie." Continue to find bigger items to cover up each lie. Talk about what we should do when we lie instead of covering up the lie with more lies.

## BELT OF TRUTH

Read Ephesians 6:14 and talk about how the belt of truth holds the armor of God securely in place. Then make this simple belt. You'll need 18 lengths of yarn that are long enough to go around your child's waist five times. Lay out the yarn and fold it over in half. Tie a knot a few inches from the folded end to form a loop. Separate the yarn into three sections and braid them. Tie a knot at the end of the braid. Wrap the belt around your child's waist and slip the knotted end through the looped end. Use the belt as a reminder to always tell the truth.

## PROTECTED

Give each family member a 1-foot-long piece of foil and have each put bite-sized pieces of carrots, potatoes, onions, and stew meat on the foil. Pour ¼ cup of barbecue sauce on top. Seal the foil and cook the pouches on your barbecue grill for an hour. Compare God's protection of Shadrach, Meshach, and Abednego in the furnace to the way the foil protected your dinner from the flames. One family member might say that the three men's characters were improved by their fiery trial just as your meal was improved by cooking. Someone else might say that the Bible story is different because the men weren't cooked by the flames.

# B·O·N·U·S
# I·D·E·A·S

## G REAT GAMES

### PAINT RELAY

Before class, photocopy and cut apart the "Paint Relay" handout (p. 165). Hang sheets of newsprint on a classroom wall at children's eye level. Also put newspaper on the floor under the newsprint. Place the *paint set, foam shapes, paintbrushes,* and a bowl of water on a chair near the newsprint.

Form teams of four and have them line up for a relay race on the side of the room opposite the newsprint and paints. Give each child on each team a section of the "Paint Relay" handout picturing what he or she will paint when it's his or her turn.

Say: **In this relay, you'll paint pictures as quickly as you can. Don't try to paint a perfect picture, just hurry to paint the item that's on your slip of paper, then walk quickly back to your team. Ready? Go!**

● The first people in line will walk quickly across the room, paint a schoolhouse, then put the *paintbrushes* down and walk quickly back to their teams.

● The second set of children will paint two trees near the schoolhouse.

● The third set of children will paint a boy and a girl in the schoolyard.

● The fourth set of children will paint a teacher near the schoolhouse.

If you have more than four children on each team, add things for them to paint, such as a jungle gym in the schoolyard, flowers near the front door of the schoolhouse, and birds in the sky. The first team to finish is the winner.

Use this game with the lessons on school. You can also adapt this idea to review the lessons on Elijah or Ezra and Nehemiah by changing the items the children are asked to paint.

### NEVER-ENDING RELAY

Make two masking tape squares on the floor on opposite sides of the room from each other. (Each square should be big enough to allow half of your class to stand in it comfortably.) Form two teams and have each team stand inside one of the squares. The side of each masking tape square facing the other square will serve as the starting line for this relay.

Ten feet away from one side of each square, place masking tape on the floor in the shape of an X. Each X should be 2 feet long. Put the *big eraser* on one of the X's.

On "go," have the first person on the team closest to the eraser run to the eraser, pick it up, run across the room, put the eraser on the other team's X, and run to the back of that team's line. Then have the first person on the next team pick up the eraser, run across the room, put the eraser on the other team's X, and run to the back of that team's line.

Make sure the teams stay in the squares to minimize the risk of collisions.

Keep playing until everyone has run at least once or until everyone is tired out.

This game works well with any lesson in this book.

# AFFIRMATION ACTIVITIES

## GOD'S IMAGE

> **Teacher Tip**
> If you have used all the paints in the *paint set,* mix 1 cup of water with 2 tablespoons of cornstarch and heat the mixture in a microwave for 1½ minutes or until it's the consistency of syrup. Stir the mixture every 30 seconds. Then stir in enough food coloring to create a brightly colored paint.

Dilute each of the watercolors in the *paint set* in ¼ cup of water. Have the children dip the surface of the *foam shapes* into the paint and stamp them onto construction paper. (The *foam shapes* will work best as stamps if they aren't soaked with paint.)

Talk about how the stamps are similar to and different from the *foam shapes.* Talk about how people are made in God's image. Ask:
- **What does it mean to be made in God's image?**
- **How were you made in God's image?**
- **How are you like God?**
- **How are you different from God?**

Tell each child how he or she is made in God's image. For example, you might tell Sarah that she shows she's made in God's image when she is patient on the playground.

Use this affirmation with any lesson in this quarter.

## ALWAYS GROWING

Get permission to plant a small garden in your church's yard. Choose a small plot of ground that can be seen from a window in your classroom—even a square foot is enough room for a few flowers. Plant easy-to-grow flower seeds such as cosmos, marigolds, or zinnias. Each week send a different child outside to water the flowers. Watch as they grow and bloom all summer long. Study Galatians 6:7-9 and talk about how God helps people grow. Give each child a bloom from the garden and say, "I can see you growing in God." If there aren't enough blooms in the garden, make some from tissue paper or construction paper or buy some cut flowers.

Use this idea any time during this quarter.

# WALL OF CANS

Help your children organize a churchwide canned-food drive. Choose a well-traveled area of your church to display the collected cans and stack the cans there to create a wall. Show the progress toward your goal by using masking tape to indicate how high, long, and wide you'd like the wall of cans to be. (For safety, make your wall no more than 2 or 3 feet high and make sure the cans are stacked so that they won't all come tumbling down.)

Use this idea with Lesson 7 on working together and Lesson 8 on kindness.

# BACK-TO-SCHOOL PICNIC

Invite the children in your class and their families to a back-to-school picnic. Have people bring their lunches in paper bags or lunch boxes. Also have families bring school supplies—such as notebooks, pencils, or crayons—to donate to children in a homeless shelter. Before you eat, sing this prayer to the tune of "Frère Jacques." Sing the first line and have the families sing the echo.

**Thank you, God,**
**(Thank you, God,)**
**For this food**
**(For this food)**
**And this time together**
**(And this time together)**
**And your love.**
**(And your love.)**

Enjoy a time of fellowship as you eat. Find out where the kids will go to school, if any of the children will be in the same class, how the children have prepared for school, and what they're excited about. End your meal by singing this second verse to the tune of "Frère Jacques." Again, sing the first line and have the children and their families sing the echo.

**Thank you, God,**
**(Thank you, God,)**

**For our schools.**
**(For our schools.)**
**Help us learn and listen**
**(Help us learn and listen)**
**Every day.**
**(Every day.)**

This is a great way to end the summer. It's a good time to welcome new children into your class and to say goodbye to children who will move to another class.

# PAINT RELAY

Make one photocopy of this handout for each team. Cut apart the sections and give the picture of the schoolhouse to the first set of children in the relay, the picture of the two trees to the second set of children, the picture of the boy and girl to the third set, and the picture of the teacher to the fourth set.

# HOBC Marketing Survey

Please help Group Publishing continue to provide innovative and exciting resources to help your children know, love, and follow Christ. Take a moment to fill out and send back this survey. Thanks!

1. What level(s) of Hands-On Bible Curriculum™ are you using?

2. How many children are in your class? adult helpers?

3. How has the size of your class changed since using Hands-On Bible Curriculum?

❑ Remained the same      ❑ Grown a lot
❑ Grown a little      ❑ Other _____

Comments:


4. When do you use Hands-On Bible Curriculum?

❑ Sunday school      ❑ Midweek group
❑ Children's church      ❑ Other (please describe) _____
_____
_____

5. What do you like best about the curriculum?

6. Is there anything about the curriculum you would like to see changed? (For example, if a certain lesson didn't work well, what specific changes would you recommend?)

7. What products would you like to see Group Publishing develop to fill specific needs in your church?

# Practical Resources for Your Children's Ministry

### The Children's Worker's Encyclopedia of Bible-Teaching Ideas

Captivate even children who have grown up in church with over 340 attention-grabbing, active-learning devotions...art and craft projects...creative prayers...service projects...field trips...music suggestions...quiet reflection activities...skits...and more. You'll find winning ideas from every book of the Bible! Directions are simple and crystal clear, so it's easy to slide an idea in any time—on short notice—with little or no preparation. And handy indexes outlining ideas by Scripture, theme, and idea style make it easy to find exactly the right idea on a moment's notice!

Old Testament               ISBN 1-55945-622-1
New Testament            ISBN 1-55945-625-6

### Quick Children's Sermons: Will My Dog Be in Heaven?

Kids ask the most *amazing* questions—and now you'll be ready to answer 50 of them! You'll get witty, wise, and biblically solid answers to kid-sized questions...and each question and answer makes a *wonderful* children's sermon. You'll know what to say when you hear questions like: "What color shoes does God like?" "Will God still love me if I don't eat my broccoli?" and more. Here's an attention-grabbing resource for children's pastors, Sunday school teachers, church workers, and parents.

ISBN 1-55945-612-4

### Incredible Edible Bible Fun
*Nanette Goings*

Roll up your sleeves for more than 50 kid-friendly, teacher-approved recipes that make learning fun *and* tasty! Each recipe ties to a simple, age-appropriate devotion or project. Your children will stir up their creations safely and quickly—you won't need any sharp knives, hot ovens, or refrigerators. And each recipe takes just 20 minutes from start to finish.

ISBN 0-7644-2001-1

### "Show Me!" Devotions for Leaders to Teach Kids
*Susan L. Lingo*

Here are all the eye-catching science tricks, sleight-of-hand stunts, and illusions that kids love learning so they can flabbergast adults...but now there's an even *better* reason to know them! Each amazing trick is an illustration for an "Oh, Wow!" devotion that drives home a memorable Bible truth. And here's a twist: You'll show your children how to share these devotions with others! **"Show Me!" Devotions** are simple enough for an all-thumbs first-grader (or teacher!), but slick enough to prompt a playground of 5th-graders to stop for the show—and then hear about Jesus.

ISBN 0-7644-2022-4

Order today from your local Christian bookstore, or write: Group Publishing, P.O. Box 485, Loveland, CO 80539.

# More Practical Resources for Your Children's Ministry

## Bible Story Crafts & Projects Children Love

Discover creative art and craft ideas that reinforce 10 Old Testament and 10 New Testament Bible stories...and help you bring the Bible to life for elementary children! And these are *fun* crafts! *Edible* crafts...*wearable* crafts...sculpting and modeling crafts...and even cooperative projects that will stay in—and decorate—your classroom! The very best ideas from outstanding teachers across the country—using easily gathered materials—now in one place! So roll up your sleeves—and tell your kids to get ready for fun as you teach them truths from God's Word in ways they'll really remember!

ISBN 1-55945-698-1

## Instant Games for Children's Ministry

*Susan L. Lingo*

Play 101 use-'em-anywhere games—and it's as easy as 1...2...3!

1. Collect 14 inexpensive, everyday items such as two Ping-Pong balls...a bag of balloons...two bandannas...things that are a snap to find!
2. Drop the items in a bag, and...
3. You're ready!

You'll always be prepared with a fun activity...action-packed game...or child-pleasing party idea! They're in the bag—ready at a moment's notice! Games come complete with instructions...rules...and quick and easy explanations so you'll have your children laughing and playing in no time!

ISBN 1-55945-695-7

## Everyone's-a-Winner Games for Children's Ministry

Turn all your kids into winners with fun, cooperative games everybody plays...and everybody wins! Here are over 100 games you can use to develop teamwork, trust, and closer friendships among your children. You'll get classroom games... gymnasium games...games for the great outdoors...and even games to play while traveling! Each game is sure-fire, no-fail fun...requires few or no supplies...and works with any size group! Lower the boom on competition, and raise the roof with fun—with **Everyone's-a-Winner Games for Children's Ministry!**

ISBN 1-55945-697-3

## Children's Ministry Guide for Smaller Churches

*Rick Chromey*

Discover practical, real-world suggestions for making the most of your small-church setting: case histories...encouraging examples...and sound advice from children's workers who are making a difference in smaller churches! Don't miss these helpful...

• Tools to help you evaluate your situation,
• Strategies for turning problems into possibilities,
• Tips for finding resources and prying money from overstretched budgets, and
• Insightful information pulled from an exclusive nationwide study of small churches.

Can you do effective children's ministry in a smaller church? Absolutely! And here's how!

ISBN 1-55945-600-0

---

Order today from your local Christian bookstore, or write: Group Publishing, P.O. Box 485, Loveland, CO 80539.